TEXAS RANGERS
in the
MEXICAN-AMERICAN WAR

TEXAS RANGERS
in the
MEXICAN-AMERICAN WAR

WILLIAM NELSON FOX

THE
History
PRESS

Published by The History Press
Charleston, SC
www.historypress.com

Front cover, top: Library of Congress; *bottom*: Library of Congress.
Back cover, top: Library of Congress; *bottom*: Library of Congress; *insert*: courtesy U.S. History Images.

First published 2023

Manufactured in the United States

ISBN 9781467153867

Library of Congress Control Number: 2022950088

Notice: The information in this book is true and complete to the best of our knowledge. It is offered without guarantee on the part of the author or The History Press. The author and The History Press disclaim all liability in connection with the use of this book.

Dedicated to my wife, who encouraged me while I buried myself in my research.

CONTENTS

CONTENTS

PREFACE

Early Texas was a mystique period that gave Texas its birth, sense of nationality, and an attachment to its ethnic identity with the rest of the world, back then and now. It was a period of intrigue, revolt, and conflict as people settled the frontier and established their identity as Texans. Texas's early history is a story of an untamed frontier dominated by hostile Indians throughout every decade of the 1800s. It was a time when people came in masses to start a new life. It is essential to know about this past and the link to today.

As an avid history buff and a longtime resident of West Texas and the Texas Hill Country, two areas steep in early Texas history, I am thankful for the opportunity to travel and research early Texas history. My passion now in retirement is to tell a reader about this early Texas history. My interest and research began years ago with one question: "How did Texas come to be?" Over the years, the more I researched, the more questions I had. "Why did so many people fight over the land called Texas?" "Why did all American-led invasions of Texas (before 1836) end in disasters?" "Why was the Alamo a heroic stand that wasn't necessary?" "Why was winning Texas independence in 1836 considered a miracle?" "Why did it take a scrappy Texas navy to save the Republic?" "Why did Texans ride into Mexico with a vengeance in 1846?" "Why did the U.S. Army fail to protect the Texas frontier?" "Why was the Texas Indian frontier so hostile to settlers in the 1850s and 1860s?" "Why was Civil War fighting on the Texas coast more remarkable than at Thermopylae?" "Why was

Reconstruction such a critical challenge in Texas?" "Why was the 1870s so terrible, with outlaws, cow thieves, and feuds?" "Why did the Texas-Comanche War last fifty years?" "Why did it take a certain army colonel to subdue the Comanches and open the final Texas frontier for settlement?"

As you can see, frontier Texas in the 1800s was an intriguing period. Even with some knowledge of early Texas history, I found there was so much I didn't know. Perhaps it will be the same for you. This presentation is one of the many stories from this early frontier period.

INTRODUCTION

The Texas Rangers watching the Lone Star flag lowered and the United States Stars and Stripes raised on that February day in 1846 did not know that their fighting with Mexico would continue. But when the call came, nothing pleased them more than an opportunity to fight the Mexicans again. Riding into Mexico, they were unwashed, unkempt hellions from Texas eager to collect on past debts and avenge the martyrs of the Alamo, Goliad, Mier, and Perote.

Veteran Texas Rangers gathered around the wood-framed Capitol building in Austin that noon on February 19, 1846. Anson Jones, the last President of the Republic of Texas, slowly lowered the Lone Star flag and handed it to J. Pinckney Henderson, the first elected Governor of Texas, as Texas officially became the twenty-eighth state of the Union. As these frontier fighters watched the Stars and Stripes rise high in the air, all their past fights with the Mexicans and Indians played out before their eyes. During its existence as a sovereign nation, the Mexican government never considered the Republic of Texas independent but rather a rebellious Mexican province. During these Texas Republic years, there were numerous border conflicts, including invasions into Texas by Mexicans and counter-invasions into Mexico by Texans, the latter resulting in disaster, imprisonment and executions.

With annexation, a real threat of war with Mexico loomed in the air. War did come, but it was an American war. After arriving in Texas with his "Army of Occupation," General Zachary Taylor mustered several frontier

Texas Ranger companies into federal service. But he left them in their respective locations guarding the Texas frontier. At the time, Taylor had no intention of involving the Texans in any fight with the Mexicans. However, after winning the first two battles of the war (fought in Texas) and preparing to cross the Rio Grande, he knew he was marching into unfamiliar terrain and about to grapple with a much larger Mexican army. General Taylor needed information about the enemy opposing him. The call for mounted Texans who knew the enemy and the terrain went out.

Even before General Taylor's call for Texas volunteers, Texan Ranger leader Jack "Coffee" Hays began contacting former Rangers and recruiting a new regiment of mounted volunteers to join the war in Mexico. Of the ten companies that would make up Hays's First Regiment of Texas Mounted Rifles, seven were led by former Texas Rangers. Jack Hays's frontier fame brought others, but only those who could shoot straight and true were accepted. Hays's men were not meek. They were rough-hewn frontier types from western Texas experienced in fighting Mexicans. But past fights had taught the Texans to expect no mercy and never to surrender. The memory of Mexican atrocities at the Alamo, Goliad, Mier, and Perote was still fresh; some had drawn beans for their lives only three years before. They had old scores to settle. They were ready for any war with Mexico.

With their skills, experience fighting the Mexican military, and knowledge of the country and the people, operating units of Texas Rangers quickly became the eyes and ears of the U.S. Army. By providing invaluable intelligence, their effectiveness marked the pace of the American offensive into Northern Mexico. The Rangers showed furious courage at Monterrey and saved General Taylor's army at Buena Vista in 1846. Then, when General Winfield Scott landed at Veracruz in March 1847, opening a campaign into Central Mexico, the Rangers once again provided valuable support to the American army in defeating the fierce Mexican guerrillas who hindered the advance of General Scott's federal troops.

Already legendary before the Mexican-American War, Texas Rangers Samuel H. Walker, Benjamin McCulloch, and John "Jack" Coffee Hays were crucial to U.S. commanders winning the war. They rode into Mexico avenging past injustices on their terms, mixing their personal goals with those of the U.S. Army. The Rangers from Texas were men who took an eye for an eye. It was a "nasty war." This is that story.

This is Texas history, reflecting the attitudes at that time and the unpleasantry of war. Were the Texas Rangers heroes or villains? It is a conclusion for you, the reader, to make.

I

COMING TO START A WAR

1

TEXAS STATEHOOD MEANT WAR

Mexico reserved the right to reclaim Texas.

On February 19, 1846, artillery boomed in Austin. As the United States Stars and Stripes rose in the air, President Anson Jones declared, "The Republic of Texas is no more!"[1] This final act moved veteran frontiersmen who were watching the flag-rising. All their past fights with the Mexicans and Indians played out before their eyes. Texas was now associated with a mighty nation, the United States. During the joyous ceremony, no one realized that the trail of bloody fighting with Mexicans and Indians that brought them to this point would continue for years.

The annexation of Texas also culminated in a series of international events between Texas, Mexico, and the United States. The Republic's status with the international community as a sovereign nation had been precarious without peace with Mexico. Even the British and French pressured Mexico to sign a treaty of recognition and peace with Texas. Then, with the government turmoil in Mexico, Santa Anna was replaced by General José Joaquín Antonio de Herrera. President General Herrera felt that Mexican intransigence was producing the worst of all worlds for the country. Herrera signed a treaty recognizing Texas's complete independence, provided that the Republic did not join the United States. But it was too late.

It was a time when American expansionists believed the United States was destined to control all the territory between the Atlantic and Pacific Oceans. What blocked this vision of "Manifest Destiny" in the West was

Map of territory in the struggle between two nations. *Courtesy U.S. History Images.*

the territories of the Republic of Mexico. And there was the question of the border between Mexico and southern Texas. Texas claimed that its border with Mexico was the Rio Grande River. By annexation, the United States inherited this claim. The Mexican government insisted that the border was not the Rio Grande but much farther north, 200 miles north, at the Rio Nueces River. The intervening disputed Trans-Nueces region (between the Rio Grande and Rio Nueces) was an uninhibited wasteland. This land had no particular economic interest to either government, and neither government defined the territory it encompassed. Still, the region became a critical pawn in the international dispute between the two nations.

Believing that the expansion of the United States was both justified and inevitable, President James K. Polk offered to forgive the $3 million in claims the United States had against Mexico if Herrera would sign over the Trans-Nueces region. Additionally, Polk offered to buy the rest of Northern Mexico for $25 million. With the Mexican government debt-ridden (in Mexico's best year, 1844, revenues had been only $20.6 million), Polk believed Mexico would find the U.S. offer irresistible. The constant state of disarray of the government in Mexico City contributed to the economic stagnation of the country and the ever-growing national debt. Then, as Polk's emissary and secret representative, John Slidell, arrived in Mexico, Polk's plans to buy Mexican territory were leaked. The Mexican press went ballistic, demanding to know who put up the for-sale sign.

Polk's heavy-handed diplomacy caused Mexicans to rally around their government, and Mexico's contending factions, still fuming over the loss of Texas, were only in agreement on their hostility toward the United States.

Left: James K. Polk, President of the United States. *Brady-Handy Collection. Library of Congress.*

Right: Zachary Taylor, Major General, U.S. Army, by Alfred M. Hoffy. *Library of Congress.*

Thus, President Herrera was in a precarious position. He wanted to avoid war, but he was in danger of being overthrown. To boost his damaged credibility, Herrera condemned the annexation of Texas as a "monstrous novelty…in insidious preparation for a long time."[2] The Mexican Senate broke off negotiations with the United States and gave Herrera authority to raise troops and prepare for war. Herrera warned the world that Mexico would mobilize its entire army and that Mexico reserved the right to reclaim Texas.

Even though Mexico's government was in disarray and unprepared to deal with either internal or external crises, there was a general feeling that Mexico was superior militarily to the North Americans.[3] Even European diplomats believed the Mexican army was superior to the American army. The American military was small and thinly spread throughout the country. President Herrera organized an army of 6,000 men and ordered General Mariano Paredes to march north to the disputed border. General Paredes had recently helped Herrera overthrow Santa Anna, sending Santa Anna into exile in Cuba. Afterward, President Herrera gave Paredes responsibility for the country's defense. However, instead of marching to the disputed territory on the border, as ordered, General Paredes led his army south to Mexico City. He overthrew Herrera and installed himself as Mexico's new president.

Even before a Texas convention could convene at Austin on July 4, 1845, to accept the American offer of annexation, the Texas government demanded a strong American military presence for protection in case the vote was for annexation. Thus, with Texas's admission into the Union nearly at hand, the Mexicans refusing to deal, and Mexican leadership in turmoil, President Polk resorted to a more drastic means to get the land he wanted by trumping up a case for war with Mexico. Polk ordered Brigadier General Zachary Taylor, who was already assembling troops at Fort Jesup, Louisiana, to march into Texas. General Taylor entered the future U.S. state with 3,900 men and orders to take his army as far as the Nueces River (the border claimed by Mexico) to guard the future state against any invasion from Mexico.

2

OCCUPATION OF TEXAS

Sent to provoke a fight.

So, with the inevitable annexation into the United States, Texans heard the roll and throb of fife and drum of an army. The American army came to Texas by land and sea to meet a Mexican army in case hostilities broke out. But it took months to scrape together an expeditionary force from the lonely military frontier posts and sleepy understaffed coastal forts across the continental United States. The Army sent U.S. Dragoons and artillery to Texas without their mounts and mules. Instead, the Army Quartermaster believed that wild Texas mustangs could be caught and broken for use, saving the government substantial money. Although the mustangs were tough and they could live off prairie grass instead of expensive feed, these little horses were about as useful as goats for pulling heavy guns. And mules had to be found and purchased, usually from Mexicans.

General Zachary Taylor arrived on St. Joseph's Island off the Texas coast on July 25, 1845. Crossing over to the little village of Corpus Christi on the south bank of the Nueces River, Taylor picked a nearby area for a camp and ordered his officers to begin training. The U.S. "Army of Occupation" gradually assembled. Most of its infantry and artillery arrived by boat from New Orleans. But he had Colonel David E. Twiggs and the U.S. Second Dragoons ride overland from Fort Jesup to join their comrades at Corpus Christi. Soon, 3,000 U.S. soldiers

Above: *Bird's-Eye View of the Camp of the Army of Occupation* near Corpus Christi, Texas, October 1845, by Charles Fenderich. *Library of Congress*.

Right: Ulysses S. Grant, Lieutenant U.S. Army. Unknown engraving. *Mexican-American War, Wikimedia Commons*.

were camped at Corpus Christi. From a bluff overlooking the beach along Corpus Christi Bay, Captain D.P. Whiting, U.S. Seventh Infantry, described the scene below. "Flapping in the Gulf breeze, rows of white canvas tents stretched toward the horizon. Blue uniformed U.S. soldiers and their horses looked as small as sand crabs. Five ships and three other vessels lie on the green waters of the bay." Not since the War of 1812 had so many American men and arms amassed at one location. Half the U.S. Army had come to Texas.[4]

Many young officers, like Robert E. Lee, Ulysses S. Grant, Jefferson Davis, Thomas Jackson (later "Stonewall" Jackson), and George B. McClellan, were about to fight together as brothers. (Two decades later, they would command large armies during the American Civil War.) As recent graduates of West Point, they were about to learn how to endure hardship, inspire troops' loyalty, and fight and win battles. Some of the young officers had opinions about why they were there. "We were sent to provoke a fight," Lieutenant Grant noted with an ironic shrug as if he were an impartial observer instead of a would-be combatant. "But it was essential that Mexico commence it."[5]

3

MEXICAN WAR BEGINS IN TEXAS

Who would be the first to start a war?

Some suspected that Taylor's army presence in Texas would incite a Mexican attack. But the Mexicans did not react to the American army arriving so close to Mexico. Then President Polk made his next move. With Mexico unwilling to come to the Nueces River to drive the invaders from what it called "her soil," Secretary of War William L. Marcy ordered General Taylor to cross the Nueces River and establish an outpost opposite the Mexican town of Matamoros. On March 11, 1846, Taylor's troops struck their tents. The troops gathered in company formation on the sands of Corpus Christi, making ready to venture off into the Trans-Nueces region (no-man's-land) that was currently buffering the American and Mexican armies. Young lieutenants and captains forming their troops on the Corpus Christi sands included James Longstreet, Edmund Kirby Smith, George G. Meade, William J. Hardee, and Braxton Bragg, to name a few.

In General Taylor's marching path to the Rio Grande were Texas's broad, sluggish rivers. But neither Taylor nor his staff had the forethought to bring pontoons for river crossings. Nine days after the army set out from Corpus Christi, Lieutenant Grant caught up with the rest of Taylor's army. He arrived dusty and exhausted on the banks of a tidal river known as the Arroyo Colorado. Having reached that river, Taylor found that Mexican soldiers were on the far shore. Not knowing how many troops were hiding in the scrub brush on the other side, General Taylor halted his army. The northern bank of the Arroyo Colorado became a scene of organized chaos, with thousands of soldiers and hundreds of mules, horses, and bellowing oxen milling around. All the while, from the other shore, there was the continuous, annoying blare of Mexican bugles, blowing nonstop unseen from behind thick scrub.

Finally, General Taylor ordered the Arroyo Colorado crossed. The Mexicans were bluffing. Taylor's army waded the stream. On March 28, 1846, his troops reached the Rio Grande River opposite Matamoros, Mexico. The Mexican and American armies now faced off on each side of the river, waiting to see who would make the first move. General Taylor constructed Fort Texas, a six-sided star with a moat encircling the earthwork structure, on the Texas side of the river.

With the arrival of the American army, General Francisco Mejia, in command across the river at Matamoros, issued a proclamation (typical for the era) lambasting the Americans for violating Mexico's territorial integrity and vowed to meet the evil presence of the conquerors with military force. However, General Mejia had no orders to fight Taylor and was too weak until reinforcements arrived. On April 11, 1846, Major General Pedro de Ampudia relieved General Mejia. General Ampudia entered Matamoros by parading noisily through the town with a 200-man escort of light cavalry. Three days later, an infantry force of 2,200 under Major General Anastasio Torrejón arrived. Mexico was mobilizing a large army at Matamoros "to sweep the Yankee heretics from their soil."[6]

The Mexicans confidently aimed their cannons across the river at General Taylor's position in Fort Texas (later named Fort Brown). Then, on April 12, General Ampudia sent Taylor an ultimatum to withdraw beyond the Nueces River or face a fight. Taylor ignored the ultimatum. On April 24, 1846, General Mariano Arista, appointed to command the Mexican Army of the North to confront the Americans, arrived in Matamoros, bringing the force facing the Americans to about 5,000 men. Meanwhile, 500 Americans inside Fort Texas sat across the river, waiting for something to happen. If attacked, their only possible help was General Taylor's 2,200 men unloading badly needed supplies on the Texas Gulf Coast, a two-day journey away.

On April 25, 1846, General Taylor received reports that Mexican troops were crossing the Rio Grande. He sent Captain Seth Thornton and two companies of the U.S. Second Dragoons upriver to investigate. The Dragoons rode through the night, traveling 40 miles in the darkness. They were drowsy, impatient, and eager to make a cursory pass through the bottomlands along the river before trotting back to tell General Taylor that the rumors were false. They were approaching the large *Rancho de Carricitos*. Captain William J. Hardee was bone-tired and cautious. Arriving at the rancho, he thought it was where they could easily be trapped—but Captain Thornton was unworried. Then, as early dawn broke, the American troopers saw angry Mexican cavalrymen riding fast toward them to the east. Thornton, Hardee, and their U.S. Second Dragoons troopers were trapped.

Thornton led a frantic charge toward the gate, as it was their only hope of escaping. The Americans' attempt to break out failed as soon as it began. Five minutes into the fight, riderless American horses galloped in circles, their empty saddles attesting to the Dragoons' decimation. Captain Thornton escaped into the chaparral unseen, while Mexican cavalrymen prevented Captain Hardee's remaining men from escaping. Hardee and his surviving men surrendered. Thornton was captured several days later and joined Hardee as a prisoner. Mexican soldiers had killed 11 Americans, wounded 6, and captured the rest. The first General Taylor heard about the fight was on April 27, 1846, when a Mexican cart rolled in carrying a badly wounded Dragoon carrying a note from General Torrejon saying that he did not have medical facilities to care for the man. Torrejon's note assured Taylor that the U.S. troopers were prisoners. The injured soldier confirmed that Captain Thornton's troopers were attacked by soldiers and not bandits. Later, on May 14, 1846, Mexico returned the captured U.S. soldiers, including Thornton and Hardee, in a prisoner exchange.

News of the "Victory over the *Gringos*" spread joy in Mexico. General Arista later bragged that he had the pleasure of being the first to start the war. As far as General Taylor was concerned, the Mexicans had brought the war to American soil, and he wrote to Washington asking for immediate reinforcements. "Old Rough and Ready" General Taylor's message to the president was: "Hostilities may now be considered commenced."[7] On May 13, 1846, Congress formally declared war on Mexico.

The Mexican-American War officially began with an artillery duel against Fort Texas across the river from Matamoros. On May 3, 1846, at 5:00 a.m., Mexican artillery opened heavy fire on the fort, and Mexican and American artillery dueled for six days. Two U.S. soldiers died in the bombardment, but that toll included fort commander Jacob Brown. The Americans could do nothing more than wait for General Taylor to rescue them.

II

EAGER FOR WAR WITH MEXICO

4

NEEDING BORDER EXPERIENCE

War was his element, and battle his playground.

After arriving in Texas, General Taylor mustered several of John Coffee "Jack" Hays's frontier Texas Rangers companies into federal service but left them in their respective locations to guard the frontier. He reluctantly accepted these Rangers into U.S. federal service to keep the Texans in the game.[8] Taylor was not interested in any Texans joining his army at the time. But he knew he would eventually need information about the enemy opposing him. He was marching into unfamiliar terrain to grapple with a much larger Mexican army. Taylor needed men who knew the countryside and the character of the inhabitants. He needed mounted men to keep his communications open and to relieve the regular dragoons of a service that they found oppressive and demanding. His dragoons were too cumbersome to perform tasks such as scouting enemy territory, screening the army's movements, and delivering important dispatches. U.S. Army Dragoons rode into battle, dismounted, and fought as infantry. And of course, the Dragoons had no experience operating along the Texas frontier. Texans had the experience Taylor needed. They knew the landscape, the people, and the culture.

Texas Ranger Samuel H. Walker had already joined Taylor's army (as a private). General Taylor knew of Walker's experience fighting Mexicans, as Walker already had a well-known reputation in military circles when the war with Mexico broke out. He was a strapping 30-year-old veteran of

Captain Walker's Expedition. *Courtesy U.S. History Images.*

wars with Comanches and Mexicans and had recently been a prisoner of the Mexicans at Mier. "War was his element," said a fellow Ranger, "the bivouac his delight, and the battlefield his playground."[9] General Taylor was impressed with Walker, and Taylor badly needed men like him to serve as scouts and couriers for his army. Taylor authorized Walker to raise a company of Texas-mounted men. Walker hastily organized 26 men whom he recruited from around Corpus Christi and Port Isabel. After being sworn into federal service on April 21, 1846, Walker's Texans patrolled Taylor's lines of communications and supply and gathered intelligence on enemy forces in the area. They carried dispatches between the two American military posts: Fort Texas at Matamoros and Taylor's encampment on the coast at Port Isabel.

When Mexican lancers crossed the Rio Grande on April 28, 1846, in force intending to isolate Taylor at Port Isabel, Walker's Texans set out to carry the news to Taylor. But to get to Taylor, the Texans had to break through a substantial Mexican screen. Twelve miles from Port Isabel, Walker and his men encountered 1,500 Mexican cavalry lancers. In the fight, his inexperienced men faltered. The Mexicans pursued Walker and his men almost to Port Isabel. Walker himself was missing and reported killed, but he later came in. Asking for volunteers, Walker, with six other men, carried the message of the Mexicans crossing the river to Taylor despite the many Mexicans along the road. Then Walker rode back through the Mexicans to tell Major Jacob Brown at Fort Texas that Taylor was safe at Port Isabel and that he (Taylor) was coming soon to his rescue. Walker's bravery quickly earned him the respect of General Taylor. Abner Doubleday, a U.S. artillery officer with the army, praised the gallant Walker, noting that despite the dangers and obstacles, Walker had successfully executed his task. Walker had rendered this service when less experienced men would probably have failed.

The intelligence that Walker provided allowed Taylor to commit his forces, leading to American victories at Palo Alto and Resaca de la Palma. On May 8, 1846, Taylor's 2,288 troops battled a Mexican army of 3,709 at Palo Alto near Brownsville. A squadron of Walker's Texans guarded

The Battle of Palo Alto. Lithograph by Sarony & Major. *Library of Congress.*

Genl. Taylor at the Battle of Resaca de la Palma. Unknown artist. *Mexican-American War, Wikimedia Commons.*

Taylor's flanks during the battle. When 800 enemy cavalrymen tried to turn Taylor's right, Walker and 20 mounted Texans pounced on the enemy, sweeping their ranks with a devastating barrage from their rifles and revolvers that forced the harried Mexican lancers to reel and flee. The Palo Alto fight ended mainly in a draw, but it was a decisive American tactical victory against a superior enemy. After the battle, the Mexican Army retreated to a deep, dried-out riverbed of dense trees and chaparral known as Resaca de la Palma.

In General Taylor's fight at Resaca de la Palma the next day, Walker's Texans probed forward and helped determine the disposition of the enemy forces. Also, during the battle, Walker's Texans escorted an artillery battery into position. During this fight with the Mexicans, Walker's horse took a bullet and tumbled to the grass. As the Ranger got untangled from his fallen mount and struggled to his feet, Walker saw a Mexican lancer bearing down on him with the shining blade of his pike pointed straight at his gut. Walker had no trouble remembering being speared once before in an Indian fight. With the elegantly uniformed cavalryman coming almost close enough to impale him, Walker toppled him with a well-placed pistol shot.

Fighting at Palo Alto and Rescas de la Palma, Walker got some of the revenge he craved against the Mexicans (but he was not through, as we will see). Walker's Texans were the only Texas unit with General Taylor at the time. General Taylor accomplished these victories through the intelligence Walker provided and by innovative positioning of flying artillery (mobile light cannons), firing grapeshot (small round balls) and canister shot (iron balls) that mowed the Mexicans down. Lieutenant Napoleon Dana, U.S. Seventh Infantry, called the victory a horrid spectacle, remarkable and brilliant. The disorganized Mexican army withdrew south of the Rio Grande after the two fights. News of Taylor's victories didn't reach Washington until May 23, 1846. Meanwhile, on May 18, 1846, General Taylor's troops occupied Matamoros, and the Mexicans continued their retreat southward into the Mexican interior.

General Taylor elected to build on his battlefield success with a deeper invasion of Mexico to solidify American control and compel the territorial concessions that President Polk wanted. However, Taylor had little intelligence concerning the enemy's location. Taylor dispatched another newly arrived volunteer company from Texas led by Texas Ranger Captain John T. Price. Price had raised a company of men from Victoria and Goliad Counties and had joined Taylor's army in May 1846, serving primarily as escorts and scouts. On May 19, 1846, Taylor sent Price's Texans and a force of U.S.

Battle of Resaca de la Palma and Battle of Palo Alto. View of two battles: (*top*) General Taylor's staff observes during the Battle of Resaca de la Palma and (*bottom*) American forces in formation at the Battle of Palo Alto. Emil Klauprecht, Lithographer. *Library of Congress.*

Dragoons to locate the retiring Mexican force. They trailed the retreating enemy for almost 60 miles before coming up on the Mexican rearguard and attacking it. In the skirmish, they suffered two wounded before returning and reporting to Taylor that General Arista was heading for Monterrey, more than 160 miles away. (Price's Texans were mustered out of federal service on June 25, 1846.)

By now, General Taylor had recognized the value of these unorthodox Texans who knew the country and the people. On April 26, 1846, Taylor called on the Governor of Texas to request two mounted regiments and two infantry regiments of Texas volunteers despite his well-known animosity toward militia units.

5

A CALL LONG WAITED FOR

Ready for any war with the Mexicans.

When John Coffee "Jack" Hays arrived at camp with his detachment of Rangers on March 18, 1846, following the Rangers' Comanche fight at Paint Rock, his men's enlistment term had expired. The next day, the Ranger unit disbanded. Hays returned to his headquarters in San Antonio, where he learned that General Taylor's army was advancing to the Rio Grande. Even before Taylor's appeal to the Texas governor for Texan volunteers, Hays's veteran Rangers had urged him to organize a regiment to fight in Mexico. Hays decided to go to Austin to discuss the matter with Governor J. Pinckney Henderson. Henderson approved the idea. Then Hays, in company with Samuel Walker, rode from Austin to Washington-on-the-Brazos with the idea of contacting former Rangers, whom he preferred as recruits. Hays began recruiting men for a new regiment. His organized mounted regiment was officially designated as the First Regiment Texas Mounted Rifle Volunteers and later referred to as Hays's First Texas Regiment, but it was known popularly as Hays's Rangers. On May 6, 1846, the *Houston Telegraph and Texas Register* reported, "All the ranging companies on our western frontier…are on the march…and having long wished for a brush with the Mexicans."[10]

At the same time, George T. Wood began raising the second requested mounted regiment in the eastern parts of Texas, designated the Second Regiment Texas Mounted Rifle Volunteers and later referred to as Wood's

Second Texas Regiment. Besides Wood's Second Texas Regiment, Albert Sidney Johnston organized another Texas regiment at Governor Henderson's request. However, the regiment's enlistment ran out before the Battle of Monterrey. Some of the men stayed to fight, and Johnston stayed serving as the inspector general of volunteers. He would later fight at the battles of Monterrey and Buena Vista.

During June and July 1846, ten companies that made up the First Regiment Texas Mounted Rifle Volunteers would join Taylor's army along the Rio Grande. Hays's First Regiment Texas Mounted Rifle Volunteers did not march to the Rio Grande in a body but rather by individual companies. The first to join General Taylor on May 23, 1846, was Benjamin McCulloch's Rangers organized in Gonzales. Robert Addison "Ad" Gillespie organized a San Antonio Ranger company, but it was July before the company joined Taylor. Hays permitted McCulloch's and Gillespie's companies to detach from his regiment, understanding that they would rejoin him when he arrived. McCulloch would later join Hays's First Regiment Texas Mounted Rifle Volunteers and lead Company A. Gillespie would join Hays's First Regiment and lead Company I, with William A.A. "Big Foot" Wallace as the first lieutenant. In detached U.S. federal service, both McCulloch's and Gillespie's companies acted as spy companies making long-range reconnaissance scoutings. They were assigned to gather intelligence concerning the enemy, the roads, and the country in the army's advance.

Meanwhile, Jack Hays continued recruiting men in Texas to fill the authorization for a mounted regiment. Besides former Texas Rangers, Hays's fame and the prospect of stirring adventure attracted others. One was Louis Haller, a clerk in a store in San Antonio. He bought a good horse, a brace of pistols, and a long knife and rode to the Rangers' camp to enlist. The first man he met near the tents was currying (grooming) a horse, and Louis asked him if he could see Major Hays. The Ranger walked to a tent and called out, "Another one, Jack!" When Hays appeared, Haller said, "Major, I'd like to join your Rangers." Many came to join Hays's regiment, but only those who could shoot straight and true were accepted. Hays looked Louis straight in the eye, said nothing, and then walked slowly around the rider and his mount, examining both. "Come with me!" Hays then commanded. Hays walked rapidly about 100 yards beyond the camp, with Haller following him on his horse. Hays pointed toward two trees about 300 yards away and said: "Jump your horse to a run, pull your pistols as you go, and put a ball into the first tree as you pass it. Circle your running horse beyond the second tree, and shoot into its trunk as you come back." Afterward, Hays led Haller back to camp. He shook hands with Louis, who climbed back on his horse and headed back toward San Antonio. A few weeks later, when Hays and his men rode to join other recruits for his regiment, Haller was not with them.[10]

Hays's First Texas Regiment incorporated so many former Rangers that it remained a Texas Ranger unit. Commanding the regiment, besides Hays, Samuel Walker was elected Lieutenant Colonel, and Michael Chevallie was elected Major. Walker resigned his captaincy in federal service to join Hays's regiment. Lieutenant John Salmon Ford transferred to Hays's staff as regimental adjutant. Ford described the regiment's commander. Hays was a short man, standing just under five feet eight and carrying barely 150 pounds on his wiry frame. He spoke and ate little; he was nervous and walked slightly stooped; his cheeks were gaunt, and his hands were thin and pale. But Jack Hays's men were not so meek. His Rangers were mostly from western Texas. They were rough-hewn frontier types. They had learned from the vaquero of South Texas that a good horse was essential. They had learned from the Comanche the fearless charge and ferocity of pursuit of the enemy. They had learned from the Lipan Apache how to read horse tracks and create deception in a fight. They were trained in marksmanship and horsemanship, skirmishing tactics, precision movements on horseback and the shock effect of the Colt revolvers. Ford best summarized the recruits: "They ride like Mexicans, trail like Indians, shoot like Tennesseans, and fight like the devil."[11]

Benjamin McCulloch's detached company was the first of Hays's First Texas Regiment to enter the war and the third company of scouts to join the army after Walker's Texans and Price's Texans. McCulloch's Rangers rode from Gonzales to Corpus Christi in just two days and then to Port Isabel, where they secured equipment, including Colt revolvers with extra cylinders for each man, but they refused army uniforms. Samuel C. Reid Jr., a scout from Louisiana with McCulloch's Rangers, described his fellow Rangers as a mob rather than a military unit. They were savage-looking men with long, matted hair and long beards dressed in everyday garments. The only uniform they wore was the infamous wide-

A Ranger of the First Regiment of Texas Mounted Riflemen Volunteers. *Courtesy U.S. History Images.*

brimmed slouched hat. They were a band of brigands.[12] Notwithstanding their ferocious outlaw appearance, there were doctors, some lawyers, and many college graduates among them. Another of McCulloch's Rangers, Jonathan Duff Brown, added that he did not recall "any ministers of the Gospel in our party."[13]

A crowd of desperate characters was the first impression U.S. regulars had of McCulloch's Rangers arriving at General Taylor's camp at Matamoros. Some wore buckskin shirts stained with tobacco and blood. They tucked their trousers into their high boots. Some wore jackets of Mexican leather and deerskin leggings and moccasins. With trail dust all over, huge beards, lean and brawny frames, and fierce eyes, they had a savage appearance. They were unwashed, unkempt hellions from Texas. Their horses were the best-groomed members of the unit and ranged from little mustangs to large American horses of every shade and color. With incomparable knowledge of horseflesh, Rangers took meticulous care of their mounts. George Wilkins Kendall, a journalist who enlisted in McCulloch's Rangers, noted that every man had a horse under him that could run for its life and save yours. Lieutenant Brackett observed with awe the firepower they could unleash armed with a pair of Colt revolvers and do so with deadly accuracy.[14] Each Ranger was a veritable arsenal on horseback, and all carried huge bowie knives, known as "Texas toothpicks."

While camped at Matamoros, McCulloch's Rangers called their quarters "Camp Maggot." The camp was downstream from the army's slaughter pens, and the refuse thrown into the river often failed to clear the banks. The Rangers used the river water for washing, drinking, and cooking; on some days, they had to wade 50 or more yards beyond the bank to avoid floating maggots.[15] After three weeks, the company was ordered back across the Rio Grande to Fort Brown. McCulloch's Rangers remained encamped opposite Matamoros until June 12, 1846, when they received orders to harass the rearguard of Mexican General Arista's retreating columns and check the condition of the road and the availability of food, water, and forage along the way.

6

OPPORTUNITY TO EXACT PUNISHMENT

A conflicted past instilled many Rangers with hatred.

The men who joined Hays's First Texas Regiment of Mounted Volunteers were eager to avenge the martyrs of the Alamo and the Goliad massacre and other Mexican atrocities, real and imagined.[16] Nothing pleased the Texans more than an opportunity to fight the Mexicans again. They were looking for an opportunity to punish Mexicans. Walter Prescott Webb explains: "From long experience with Mexico, the Texans had come to distrust every word and deed of the race. The affair at the Alamo had taught them to expect no mercy; the massacre of Fannin's men in violation of all law had taught them distrust of Mexican honor; the fate of the Mier prisoners in Perote prison had taught them never to surrender, and the victory of San Jacinto taught them contempt for Mexican valor."[17] Only three years before, some had drawn beans for their lives and worked in the streets in chains, footsore and nearly starved. A.J. Sowell, whose cousin was shot after drawing a black bean at Hacienda Salado, remarked that many Rangers had old scores to settle with the Mexicans. They wanted revenge. In North Texas, the publisher of the *Northern Standard* in Clarksville believed all Americans should feel that way and wrote: "We trust that every man of our army, as he points his rifle or thrusts his bayonet, will think of his countrymen martyred at the Alamo, at Goliad, and Mier."[18] The Texans welcomed the call to fight Mexicans.[19]

The Texans' relationship with Mexicans was noted by arriving U.S. soldiers. Lieutenant Ulysses S. Grant pointed out that the hostilities between Texans and Mexicans were so great that neither was safe in the neighborhood of the other. Understandably, the Rangers' reputations had preceded them into battle. Lieutenant Rankin Dilworth, U.S. First Infantry, commented that the Mexicans dreaded the Texans more than they did the devil, and they had a good reason for it.[20] Many thought the Texans were too prone to kill Mexicans on any pretext. Many Texans nursed grudges as old as a decade, and they were motivated more by private vendettas than patriotism. Samuel Chamberlain, U.S. First Dragoons, called them "packs of human bloodhounds."

Now in federal service, General Taylor listed his intelligence requirements in his orders to Benjamin McCulloch: locate and determine the condition of the Mexican army, analyze the route in terms of trafficability for the artillery, and determine if the course was capable of providing subsistence along the way.[21] But that wasn't the only mission Captain McCulloch had in mind. He added a personal mission: to search for Mexican Brigadier General Antonio Canales (called the "Chaparral Fox"). Canales had made bloody cross-border raids into Texas and was a bitter enemy of the Texans. To strike the Chaparral Fox in the hills and slaughter his band was a thing above all others that McCulloch desired to do.[22] The dual mission probably seemed very efficient to McCulloch, but had General Taylor known beforehand of McCulloch's intent, Taylor might not have approved. While Taylor desired Canales's capture, his primary focus was defeating the Mexican army, not chasing the Texans' enemies.

On June 12, 1846, McCulloch's Rangers began their concerted forward reconnaissance patrols in guiding Taylor's army columns into unfamiliar territory. Thirty-five Rangers struck out across the desert, hoping to obtain a fight with General Canales to settle the score for Mier, but the Chaparral Fox was not in his lair. Then McCulloch's Rangers rode southeast toward Linares to gain information for General Taylor on the number and disposition of the enemy and to ascertain if a passable southern approach to Monterrey would support the march of a large division with artillery and wagons. Aware of possible observation by Mexican spies, McCulloch's Rangers feinted toward Reynosa and then cut cross-country to the Linares Road after nightfall. After finding that direction was impassable for the expedition's logistical and artillery trains, they returned to report their findings. The Rangers established a temporary camp with the U.S. First Infantry at Reynosa. (Samuel C. Reid Jr. describes the reconnaissance mission in June 1846 in *The Scouting Expeditions of McCulloch's Texas Rangers*.)

McCulloch's Rangers spent ten days in the interior of the enemy country, traveling not less than 250 miles. They never took off their coats, boots, or

Group of Texas Rangers riding in Mexico. Anonymous drawing. *Texas Ranger Division, Wikimedia Commons*.

spurs from when they left Matamoros until they reached Reynosa.[23] The Texans' region-specific capabilities made them uniquely suited to shape General Taylor's scheme of maneuvers throughout the invasion. In one instance, which revealed the advantage of previous border experience during the Texas Republic's many wars against Mexico, McCulloch's reconnaissance party leveraged cultural familiarity against an enemy patrol. Before opening fire, the Ranger captain first deceived them by hailing them in Spanish. Capturing a dispatch carrier this way, he translated a captured map and questioned local civilians, which yielded intelligence on the shortage of water and forage ahead. Speaking the Spanish language represented another of the Texans' unique skills. All of this led General Taylor to express, in a way uncharacteristically generous for a regular army officer speaking of disdained volunteers, that the services rendered by McCulloch and his men were of the highest importance.

Meanwhile, General Taylor moved his army upriver about 30 miles to Camargo, conveniently reachable by steamboat from Port Isabel and Matamoros. Camargo was an ideal jumping-off point for Taylor's objective: Monterrey, 125 miles to the southwest. As soon as McCulloch's Rangers arrived, Taylor ordered them to conduct a scout for the best route to Monterrey. There were two routes: via Cerralvo and Marin or China and Caderita. Again, with a dual purpose in mind, McCulloch decided to reconnoiter the China route first. Walter Prescott Webb notes that McCulloch chose the China route first because of a rumor that Juan N. Seguín was in China and McCulloch wanted to capture him.[24] Seguín joined the Texans in the Texas Revolution in 1836; however, he switched to the Mexican side when Mexican General Adrián Woll invaded Texas in 1842. The Texans never forgave Seguín for his betrayal. Brigadier General William J. Worth, one of Taylor's division commanders, granted permission to eliminate Seguín if found. The force departed Camargo on August 3,

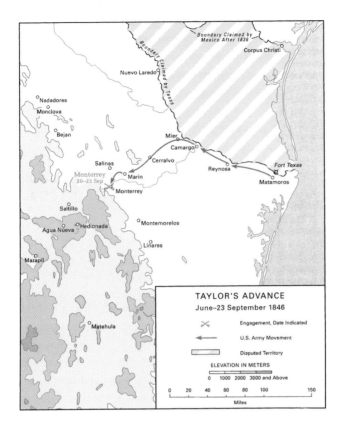

Map of Taylor's advance into Mexico, June through September 23, 1846. *Courtesy U.S. Army. Center of Military History, CMH Pub. 73-1.*

1846, in the direction of China, looking for Seguín. They didn't find Seguín but managed to capture four of his men. McCulloch rejoined Taylor's army on August 9, 1846. McCulloch's dual missions had benefits. His extended reconnaissance cleared the area of Mexican guerrilla forces who fled to avoid combat with the Rangers. However, McCulloch's actions also demonstrated the willingness of volunteer forces to act independently, seeking to achieve their aims, whether of the regular army commanders or not.

By late August 1846, Wood's Second Texas Regiment mounted companies had consolidated with Taylor's force at Camargo. Although lacking in frontier experience, these men shared the aggressiveness shown by Hays's western Texas men, and many of them had experience fighting the Mexicans. Taylor's combined army was now halfway to Monterrey, Taylor's strategic objective. As for the Texans, General Taylor gave them definite missions: McCulloch's and Gillespie's companies came under Taylor's control as intelligence gatherers, with Wood's Second Texas Regiment acting as force protectors for the marching army.

III

TEXAS RANGERS LED THE WAY

EYES AND EARS OF THE U.S. ARMY

Leading the army to Monterrey.

Major Jack Hays and his First Regiment Texas Mounted Rifle Volunteers mustered into U.S. federal service in June 1846 and marched off to the Mexican-American War. Hays received his commission as Colonel of the regiment along with orders to ascertain the operations of the enemy's army and to capture or destroy all armed parties.[25] His orders were to march 130 miles southwest of Matamoros, take a circuitous course, then join the main army, which would be en route to Monterrey. Riding with Hays, F.A. Lumsden of the *New Orleans Picayune* wrote on August 5, 1846, that General Taylor, it seems, intended to give the Rangers a chance to get into a scrape and then get out of it as best they may and that the regiment was about 700 strong.[26] To command the Texas Division, comprising Hays's First Texas Regiment and Wood's Second Texas Regiment, Texas governor J. Pinckney Henderson took a leave of absence. Upon its consolidation in mid-September 1846, the Texas Division was at its full strength at about 1,100 men.[27]

Already the first units of General Taylor's advancing army were marching from Matamoros up the Rio Grande to Reynosa, Camargo, and onto Cerralvo northwest of China across the San Juan Valley. By September 12, Taylor's consolidated force encamped at Cerralvo, poised to strike Monterrey, and where Hays's Rangers joined Taylor. General Taylor began marching his army out of Cerralvo toward Monterrey in sections at one-day intervals. Hays's First Texas Regiment rode parallel to the main column. At the same time, Hays and individual Ranger units from the regiment scouted ahead of Taylor's marching army.[28] Hays scouted from China to the west of Cadereyta and then south to Monterrey, rejoining Taylor on September 17, 1846, at Marin. On this scout, Hays had completed yet another semicircular movement by marching near Monterrey and then back to Marin. Again, Hays's maneuvering prevented the enemy from attacking the slower-moving army. Other senior military leaders began to notice the service Hays's Rangers provided. In a message to Washington, General W.H. King wrote that the Rangers were not only the eyes and ears of Taylor's army but also its right and left arms.[29]

On September 17, 1846, General Taylor issued orders for the final advance on Monterrey, stating that the Texas-mounted troops would lead the army's advance[30] Showing Taylor's growing confidence in the Texans leading the American column, his army marched toward the prize of Monterrey. Most of the First and Second Texas Regiments moved as intact regiments, except for Benjamin McCulloch's Rangers and another led by Robert Gillespie, whom General Taylor dispatched as scouts. During this march, Hays's First Texas Regiment, guarding the army's southern flank, skirmished against a larger Mexican force near Marin, losing three men. Returning intense fire, the Rangers staggered the Mexicans, who retreated in great confusion. Though just a skirmish, this engagement further underscored the lethality of the Texans' Colt revolvers.

About this time, McCulloch's and Gillespie's independent companies rejoined Hays's First Texas Regiment. General Taylor continued to employ First Texas and Second Texas per their specific skills. Hays's First Texas Regiment ranged well in advance in enemy territory, operating independently. On these reconnaissance forays, Hays and his Rangers not only successfully provided valuable intelligence, but their counter-guerrilla actions, some officially authorized and some not, also denied the enemy intelligence regarding Taylor's forces and prevented Taylor's marching troops from being surprised by the enemy. As for Wood's Second Texas Regiment, General Taylor used them as mounted escorts for his advancing columns of infantry, artillery, and supply.

The American army marching from Cerralvo arrived in the hamlet of Marin, 20 miles northeast of Monterrey, in separate brigade columns over the next few days. The army resumed its march on September 18, 1846, with a

Heights of Monterrey from Saltillo Road. Taylor's army marching toward Monterrey from the west. By D.P. Whiting, Captain, Seventh Infantry. *Courtesy Library of Congress.*

Texan vanguard of Gillespie's company and McCulloch's company, followed by Hays's First Texas Regiment and Wood's Second Texas Regiment. The Ranger regiments were followed by three U.S. infantry divisions and several state volunteer regiments. The consolidated weight of the American army now advanced toward its objective. Ranger Captain Walter P. Lane, riding with Hays's First Texas Regiment, recalled the invasion force was like an ocean swell marching to the outskirts of Monterrey.

At sunrise, on September 19, 1846, General Taylor, accompanied by his staff, rode out to look at their objective and the fortifications around Monterrey with an escort of U.S. Dragoons and two companies of Texas Rangers led by Jack Hays. Emerging from the woodlots north of the city, they came onto a broad plain of cornfields and saw grazing cattle and a few farmers' *jacales* (huts). Taylor and his staff rode up and joined Hays at the head of the column. As the morning sun climbed, fields of corn, sugarcane and fruit trees added to the sense of repose. The observers saw their objective for the first time. In the distance was the Citadel that the Americans dubbed the "Black Fort" because of its dark, 30-foot-high stone walls. It stood approximately 1,000 yards north of the city. Also defending the northeast was an earthwork, La Teneria, and a fortification known as Fort Diablo. To the west were two fortified defensive positions. Independence Hill, 800 feet

Major General Z. Taylor. Engraved by William and J.T. Howland. *Library of Congress.*

high, held two defensive structures, Fort Libertad and the Bishop's Palace. Federation Hill, 400 feet high, had a redout, Fort Soldado. The Saltillo Road ran between the two hills.

While the Americans admired the beautiful setting, a bugle blared in the city, and a regiment of Mexican lancers rode out. Jack Hays immediately ordered his men to the front, forming them into sections of fives. Hays's

Rangers then moved toward the lancers at a brisk trot. Suddenly, the Mexican lancers wheeled and retreated. Hays suspected it was a ruse to entice them within a cannon shot of the Citadel. Hays halted his force. At that instant, a cannon boomed, and a ball fell in front of them.[31] More round shots then belched rapidly from the Citadel. For the Texans, this was a challenge. Rangers rode single and rapidly, taking turns taunting the Mexicans by riding in circles closer and closer to the Citadel, vying with one another as to who could ride closest to the danger and escape. They rode zigzagging to avoid cannon shots, defying the Mexican gunners and timing their moves to when the gunners were shifting their pieces to compensate for range and direction. Their proximity provoked the enemy's fire, but the Mexicans might as well have attempted to bring down skimming swallows as those racing daredevils.[32] Many of their balls were directed very well, yet no one was hurt. Every cannon firing received a robust response of three cheers and the waving of hats. It was such huzzahing General Taylor said he had never heard. The Texans proved their spunk by the utter carelessness with which they received the enemy's shot.[33] Then General Taylor indignantly ordered the play to cease. Hays's Rangers fell back out of range, and Taylor and his staff were already countermarching.

Nightfall and heavy rain caused Colonel Hays to go into camp. Hays's Rangers had no food, coats, blankets, or supplies. They rode into a small farmyard and immediately began to scramble for chickens and pigs. The Rangers lit fires to barbecue the meat, but as Mexican cannon fire rained down, the Rangers extinguished the coals. Finding unshelled corn, the Rangers munched on that. (In fact, during the fighting around Monterrey, the Rangers lived exclusively on raw green corn.) As the Rangers slept wet, cold, and hungry on the rain-saturated ground, they would awake at the slightest noise and grab their rifles. Sleep was nearly impossible.[34] As for General Taylor's regular troops, Taylor ordered his army to encamp in a spring-fed grove of live oak and pecan trees. His troops dubbed it Walnut Springs.

8

LEADING THE ADVANCE

Courageous men, singularly careless of their own lives.

As the army bivouacked at Walnut Springs, Texas Ranger Ad Gillespie accompanied army engineers to reconnoiter the city and study its defenses. Monterrey was built on a plain on the northern side of the San Juan River. Running east and west, the city of Monterrey was a mile long. North and south, the city was a half-mile wide. Hedging the town on the south and east was the Santa Catarina River. The streets were regular, and the buildings were made of hewn stone. The Sierra Madre Mountains spurs crept close to the city and limited the plain to the north. In the city, a network of fortified defenses awaited the Americans. Every street was barricaded, and parapet walls on the buildings' flat rooftops transformed the structures surrounding Monterrey's Main Plaza into defensive structures from which Mexican infantry could rain down destruction on American troops.

Taylor had under his command less than 6,000 troops; half of these troops were state volunteers, including the Texas Division. In his path stood 7,000 Mexican regulars and 3,000 irregulars behind commanding fortifications and prepared defensive positions in Monterrey. Taylor had no battering train and insufficient field artillery. However, the Mexicans had mistakenly fortified all these strong points about the city, but these strong points didn't support one another. They could be attacked separately and reduced piecemeal. But the heights around the city had to be taken first.[35] That evening, Taylor finalized

Monterrey, House-top Main Plaza. The main plaza from a rooftop is part of the defense of Monterrey by D.P. Whiting, Captain, Seventh Infantry. *Library of Congress.*

his attack plan. Deploying his forces in a double envelopment of Monterrey, General Worth's Second Brigade, reinforced by Hays's Rangers (a combined force of nearly 2,700 men), would attack from the west. At the same time, Taylor would conduct diversions against the city's defenses on the east. Worth was to cut the Saltillo Road in the west to prevent reinforcements and cut off the enemy's supply lines. The plan was for Worth to secure Federation Hill and Independence Hill before launching the final assault on the city. General Taylor held Wood's Second Texas Regiment in reserve to gallop to the rescue should Worth get in a jam. Worth's force, in addition to the U.S. regulars and two companies of flying artillery, included McCulloch's and Gillespie's companies, along with six companies of "dismounted" Hays's First Texas Regiment under the command of Major Michael Chevallie.[36]

On September 20, 1846, General Worth's division set out for the western approach to the city, with Hays's Rangers taking the lead. Hays led his 250 men "by fives." Worth's division followed Hays's Rangers. They moved down Marin Road and then moved off to the right, crossing north of Monterrey. To many thoughtful men in the following army, it seemed odd to do a flank march while the enemy watched from the Citadel. The leading Rangers rode through the chaparral and cornfields, where the fine tassels brushed the Rangers' full beards and handlebar mustaches. They crossed the Monclova Road and arrived at the spur of a hill near Independence Hill. Hays halted his command and sent some pickets forward. Then Hays and Captain McCulloch climbed the hill to reconnoiter. A few minutes later, General Worth and his staff members, including a young engineer staff officer named Robert E. Lee, conducted a final assessment of the daunting fortifications of Independence Hill. After making their observations, the officers descended the hill.

Hays selected a detachment of scouts and rode along with General Worth and Colonel P.F. Smith. The battalion followed slowly behind them. Following a trail leading west toward Saltillo Road, the Mexicans fired on Hay's advanced group from an ambush. Then a battery on Independence Hill added a deluge of shells. When the Mexican batteries opened fire, the Texans' horses became unmanageable, not accustomed to loud shell explosions. Ranger Samuel C. Reid Jr.'s horse pitched him out of his saddle. With a foot hung in the stirrup, he held on to his horse's mane for dear life while his horse galloped blindly for about 100 yards before Reid could pull himself back up.

Then a Mexican cavalry detachment appeared. With the advance unit being heavily outnumbered and in danger of being cut off, Hays ordered a retreat. After escorting the general back to his column, Jack Hays returned just as the Mexican lancers moved forward. Hays led his Rangers in a charge that scattered the Mexican lancers. Then the Rangers turned and poured such an intense fire into the Mexican force that had ambushed them, and those Mexicans retreated as well. Not a Texan was wounded. In the fight, one of Hays's men had his horse killed under him, but the rider hit the ground on his feet and stood over the body of his horse, firing at the charging Mexican cavalrymen. Seeing the young Ranger's predicament, Lieutenant John McMullin raced back in the face of almost sure death and swung the valiant Ranger up behind him while lead whistled close to them.[37]

On September 21, 1846, Second Lieutenant George G. Meade rode close to General Worth as part of the Topographical Corps, the general's indispensable guide to the landscape and defenses. Meade was famished. He endured a rainy night with the rest of the American force. He had slept as best he could, wrapped in his trusty cloak. The lack of campfires had prevented the troops from cooking even a simple evening meal. Now his stomach rumbled, and a deep chill lingered in his bones. As he rode, the twin summits loomed above Meade's left: Independence Hill was close, and Federation Hill was on the far side of the river. At 6:30 a.m., hellfire rained down from the fortified sanctuaries. One passing cannonball was so accurate that it whooshed within two feet of Meade's pant leg and almost crushed the nearby General Taylor. The Mexicans helped out by using solid rounds that lacked explosive charges. The balls of iron were more of a nuisance to the Americans than anything else but a reminder to look lively and pay attention.[38]

General Worth's flanking movement took the Americans beyond effective artillery range. Mounted Texans served as the advance guard at the front of the column of three infantry units and two flying artillery units, including James "Pete" Longstreet's Eighth and Napoleon Dana's Seventh. They were moving toward the Saltillo Road. Dawn appeared and, with it, the Mexicans. The Jalisco Lancers, more than 200 strong, were supported with some 1,500 infantry to contest the Americans' approach. Captain McCulloch and his Rangers were about 600 yards in advance of General Worth and his division. The two opposing mounted forces (McCulloch's Rangers and the Mexican lancers) stood motionless, taking each other's measure. With their nimble and spirited horses, the Mexicans sat in brilliant uniforms on their richly embossed saddles. Each Mexican cavalryman had a pennon waving from his lance. "They were good horsemen, mounted on lively steeds and made the most beautiful spectacle," wrote Sergeant Buck Barry.[39] Standing over 200 yards away, their well-executed movements created very little noise. Leading the Mexican force was an officer with a long black mustache and splendid military bearing. He was Lieutenant Colonel Juan Nájera.

Jack Hays rode out in front of his Rangers and toward the Mexican officer. Hays had a saber in his hand. After covering almost half the distance and midway between the opposing forces, Hays bowed to the Mexican officer. In Spanish, Hays challenged the officer to a duel. The Mexican colonel doffed his headgear and bowed his acceptance. Hays's Rangers knew that Hays was not skilled with a saber, but they noticed that he had a pair of revolvers in his belt. Hays walked his mount directly toward the Mexican colonel. The Mexican's horse seemed to dance as his gallant master rode forward to meet the Ranger. When the two officers were about 40 yards apart, the lancer officer, standing in his stirrups and with his long saber at rest, charged. Dropping his saber, Hays snatched a revolver. Lying forward on his horse, Hays fired from under his horse's neck. The ball knocked the Mexican lancer officer from his saddle, killing him. Hays then spurred his horse toward his men, shouting, "Dismount! Get behind your horses! Here they come, boys! Give 'em hell!"[40]

Sergeant Barry wrote: "They charged us like mad hornets and were among us. They fought through our line, formed up in our rear and charged through the line again, formed in front and charged through our line a third time. I have never called a Mexican a coward since. They left many of their dead among us. We had only one man killed but many wounded. We killed about eighty, but we should have done better, as we only had to shoot them down a few feet from behind our horses. We had shot our muzzle-loading guns empty, and they had charged us so fast that we had not time to load again."[41]

After the lancers' charge, Jack Hays dismounted five Ranger companies as more of the enemy advanced to prevent the Americans from securing the Saltillo Road. He directed some men to hide in a cornfield on the left. McCulloch's Rangers mounted in front were ordered to feign a retreat if attacked again. When two regiments of Mexican cavalry charged, McCulloch and his men began drawing back slowly. The Mexicans raced into Hays's ambush. Hays's Rangers poured volleys of well-aimed rifle fire into the Mexicans at a distance of 10 to 20 yards. Then McCulloch's Rangers wheeled around and charged back into the Mexican ranks firing their Colt revolvers. McCulloch's Rangers crashed into the Mexican cavalry. The close-quarter fighting became desperate with swords, knives, pistols, and lances. But the Rangers proved more than a match for the Mexican lancers. The Texans used their Colt revolvers and bowie knives to murderous effect. At one point, McCulloch became cut off from his men, but he put spurs to his horse and returned to his command unscratched.

Lieutenant Longstreet led his U.S. Eighth Infantrymen forward as the Mexicans prepared for another charge. At the same time, Colonel James Duncan's U.S. Second Artillery battery of six-pounders wheeled forward and started pouring shots into the Mexican formations with highly accurate canister rounds. The carnage was instant, maiming and killing men and horses. Blood, lances, and plumed stovepipe shako hats littered the ground. The Mexican attack had been nothing less than a suicide charge. The lancers tumbled from saddles by the dozens. The Mexicans suffered 100 dead and more wounded, including the lancers' commander, Lieutenant Colonel Nájera.

Rangers are routing the Mexicans.
Courtesy U.S. History Images.

The fight lasted only 15 minutes. The Mexican survivors retreated to the relative safety of the Bishop's Palace on Independence Hill. General Worth, pleased with the skill he saw displayed by the Rangers in this engagement, pronounced it a beautiful maneuver and continued his advance. By 8:15 a.m., General Worth had severed the Saltillo Road and blocked the arrival of any Mexican reinforcements.[42]

As the Americans resumed their march, General Worth's column came under heavy fire by Mexican gunners from the two hills, Federation Hill and Independence Hill. Although the barrage caused few casualties, Worth's next move was to silence these guns. His first objective was Federation Hill. Worth sent 300 Texans supported by the U.S. Fifth Infantry and held the U.S. Seventh Infantry in reserve, a total of 860 men, to attack the hill. A mad race began between the American troops and the Texans to see who would be the first to reach Fort Soldado atop Federation Hill. Captain C.F. Smith's U.S. Fifth Infantry troops and the Texans forded the Santa Catarina River and began clawing their way up Federation Hill's rocky slope. The western face was steep, offering little cover, and the Texans and the U.S. infantrymen made the treacherous climb directly in the face of enemy artillery and musket fire. Five hundred Mexican soldiers were manning the earthworks just below the crest of the hill. General Worth ordered the U.S. Seventh Infantry to move forward and reinforce the attacking force.

Screaming their defiance, the Texans charged up Federation Hill. The fury of the Texans' charge drew the focus of the Mexicans' attention and the heaviest fire, allowing the American infantry to advance. Captain Ad Gillespie was the first to mount the earthen walls of Fort Soldado, closely followed by the Fifth and Seventh U.S. Infantry soldiers. The Mexican line crumbled and fell back. The Mexican retreat turned into a rout as they abandoned their artillery pieces and fled. The American infantry turned around captured artillery pieces, bringing the enemy under fire with their guns. The Texans raced after the fleeing Mexicans. Surviving Mexicans fled across the Santa Catarina River to the safety of Independence Hill. When the fight was over, the Texans earned the grudging respect of the proud U.S. infantry regulars. One of the men from the U.S. Fifth Infantry pulled a piece of chalk from his pocket and wrote on one of the cannons, "Texas Rangers and U.S. Fifth Infantry."[43]

Now Independence Hill needed to be taken. Posted as an observer from a position in a tree, with cannonballs flying around him, a young Ranger reported that the Mexican infantry on Independence Hill showed no sign of moving, then asked if he could come down. "No, sir. Wait for orders,"

Colonel Jack Hays replied, promptly forgetting about the man. Then remembering that the Ranger was still in the tree, Hays shouted, "Holloa, where are the Mexicans?" The Ranger reported, "Going back up the hill," not knowing who had asked the question. "Well, hadn't you better come down from there?" "I don't know," the Ranger said. "I am waiting for orders!" "Well, then, I order you down." Realizing it was Colonel Hays, the Ranger came down without waiting to be told twice.[44]

By nightfall on September 21, 1846, General Worth controlled Federation Hill. Throughout the night, American artillery fired from captured Federation Hill, dueling with the Mexican guns on Independence Hill.

9

FURY OF THE TEXANS' CHARGE

Charging like devils, yelling like Comanches.

The Bishop's Palace stood on the eastern end of Independence Hill, a stone, castle-like fortress bristling with cannons. Monterrey's other western defense was the earthen fortification, Fort Libertad, on the hill's west end. The western face of Independence Hill was so steep and rugged that the Mexicans did not bother to post sentries. Despite the rough terrain and challenging climb, Colonel Hays convinced General Worth that they could surprise the Mexicans. Worth ordered Colonel Hays and Lieutenant Colonel Thomas Childs to lead a brigade of infantry and artillery in a storming party and wrest Independence Hill from enemy control.[45]

Before they attacked Independence Hill, torrential rain fell, and fatigue had won over hunger. The troops tried to get some rest before commencing the attack. The torrential rain swept dirt and gravel against some of the Rangers resting before going into battle again. They had not slept for three nights and had been riding and fighting almost continuously for nearly three days. When a stone rolled against a man, he would jerk awake and sit up holding his rifle, but he would soon doze off again. Jack Hays was not sleeping. He was up, touching certain men on the shoulder, assembling them. There was work to do before attacking Independence Hill. After midnight, Hays led these men in single file from the camp. Across the boggy cornfields and toward Independence Hill, the little column followed Hays. At the base of the hill, Colonel Hays dropped down on his hands and knees in the mire.

There the Rangers waited for the enemy picket to be relieved. Now, they had only to wait until the newly posted sentry became a little drowsy. The Mexican picket was seized, prodded tenderly by a bowie knife held against his back, then forced to lead the Rangers to the other pickets. In this manner, the squad captured all the pickets near the base of Independence Hill.[46]

At 3:00 a.m., the assault on Independence Hill began. The wind was howling. It had turned colder, and it was raining. The order came to move forward. The attacking force numbered some 200 Texans and 300 U.S. infantrymen. They split into two assault columns. Under the command of Texas Ranger Samuel Walker, one column climbed the southwest face of the hill. The other column, led by Ben McCulloch, tackled the even more imposing northwest face. Jack Hays accompanied McCulloch's men. Overturned stones frequently rolled down the mountain, but the storm deadened the noise. Projecting crags were less difficult to ascend than the perpendicular ledges of rock. Fissures in the crags enabled the men to gain footholds.

The storm and the stiff, cold west wind helped mask the noise of their approach. The Texans had climbed within 100 yards of Fort Libertad on the western summit of Independence Hill before the Mexicans spotted them. Then the Texans charged, screaming and firing. Jack Hays scrambled up on the wall, a single-shot pistol in one hand and a revolver in the other. Captain Gillespie stood on the sandbags. In jumping over, Ad Gillespie staggered awkwardly from the thud of a bullet. Herman Thomas, a lad from Baltimore, fell at the base of the wall. The rest of the Rangers sprang over the wall, grappling, stabbing and slashing at the enemy.

Soon, enemy survivors were fleeing toward Bishop's Palace. Not pursuing, the Rangers stood silent. Ad Gillespie was mortally wounded and lay bleeding with a stomach wound. Gillespie and Thomas had fought their last battle. Gillespie passed his sword to Lieutenant G.H. Nelson and told him to lead the company. Although mortally wounded, Gillespie found the strength to rally his men. Still leading by example, he reportedly said: "Boys, place me behind that ledge and rock…and give me my revolver. I will do some execution on them before I die."[47] Gillespie lived 22 hours in agony from pain and thirst. (The Texas legislature took land from Bexar and Travis Counties and created a new county in 1848, named in Gillespie's honor.)

Before attacking Bishop's Palace, Hays proposed a plan to General Worth to advance a company of dismounted Louisiana Dragoons and then have them feint a retreat to catch the charging Mexicans in a trap. General Worth agreed with Hays's plan. Hays and his Texans moved to concealed

Storming of Independence Hill at the Battle of Monterrey. Kelloggs & Thayer Lithograph. *Library of Congress.*

positions on both sides of the hill. The Louisiana Dragoons advanced, fired a volley, and then made a hasty retreat as planned. The ruse worked. The Mexicans poured out of Bishop's Palace in pursuit of the retreating Dragoons. American artillery fired a well-coordinated volley before the American infantrymen advanced with lowered bayonets. The Texans then added to the confusion by opening fire on the exposed Mexican flanks from their concealed positions along both sides of the hill. Surviving Mexicans ran back to Bishop's Palace and slammed shut the heavy doors. James Duncan's Company A, U.S. Second Artillery, a light artillery battery, came up and soon blew open the doors. The U.S. infantry and Texans rushed into Bishop's Palace.

The fight for Bishop's Palace became long and bloody. One eyewitness remembered: "The Texan Rangers are the most desperate men in battle that I ever heard of. They charged up to the breastworks, dismounted, and rushed over on foot, with a sword in hand....[Ranger Samuel W. Chamber] got over the breastworks, obtained a foothold on a 13-pounder, and deliberately took aim with his 'five-shooter,' firing with great effect and cursing the Mexicans."[48] Chamber escaped without a wound. Fighting was hand-to-hand. "Steel clashed against steel. Muskets came down on heads with a sickening 'thud,' scattering brains and blood."[49] The Mexicans fought

Monterrey from Independence Hill in the rear of Bishop's Palace as it appeared on September 23, 1846 (looking east), by D.P. Whiting, Captain, Seventh Infantry. *Library of Congress.*

desperately as the Americans forced their way into the palace. When an officer shouted, "Throw yourselves flat," a howitzer fired a double load of canisters into the remaining Mexicans. The fight was over. The remaining defenders began throwing down their arms. Some were leaping from windows and running down the hill toward the city. General Worth had removed the enemy from the western approach to the town. Now the fight for the city of Monterrey could begin.

10

BATTLE FOR MONTERREY

Street fighting becomes appalling.

Early the following morning, September 23, 1846, the American assault on the city of Monterrey began with coordinated attacks from both the west and the east. The Texans led the attack. They had experience fighting in Mexican-style towns with narrow streets, a central square, and thick-walled buildings with parapets lining the flat roofs. As the fight began, a thunderstorm broke. The dismounted Texans ran up the streets in the pouring rain. James "Buck" Barry remembered using crowbars and sledgehammers to punch holes in stone walls to move from one house to the next. "Often, there was only a single wall between the Texans and Mexicans, so as soon as the Texans battered a hole through the wall, the Mexicans would commence shooting at random through it. It was nothing strange for the muzzles of the Texans' and Mexicans' guns to clash as both tried to shoot through the hole simultaneously."[50] The process was tedious and time-consuming. In approaching a Mexican artillery street barricade, the Texans would mount rooftops and shoot at any foolish Mexican artillerymen who came near their guns. Other Texans moved from one building to the next using accurate and deadly rifle fire.

Hays and a force of U.S. Regulars and Rangers attacked down Calle de Monterrey. Samuel Walker led another mixed force, paralleled Hay's force, and attacked down Calle de Iturbide. Samuel Reid remembered the ferocity of the battle that rainy September 23, 1846. If a street barricade proved a

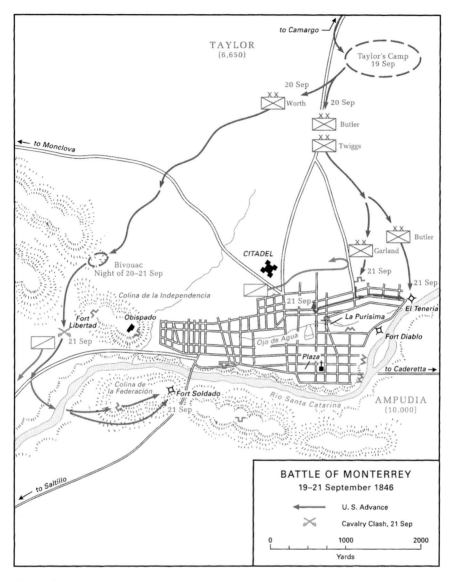

Map of Battle of Monterrey, September 19–21, 1846. *Courtesy U.S. Army. Center of Military History, CMH Pub. 73-1.*

problem against the combined attack, they would move from house to house or break through the adobe walls to gain a flank position. If this tactic failed, the other advancing column on the street, moving parallel, was signaled to bypass the barricade and then come back and fire on its rear. The street fighting became appalling. Artillery raked both sides of the streets. Doors

Charging at Monterrey, by Frederick A. Ober. *Battle of Monterrey, Wikimedia Commons.*

were forced open and walls battered down. The fight was room to room and house to house.[51] The Texans and U.S. regulars gained the housetops using ladders and poured a rain of bullets from the rooftops on the enemy. Samuel Reid said, "It was a strange and novel scene of warfare."[52] The Texans and U.S. regulars assaulted the city in a pincer movement designed to force Mexican resistance toward the center of the town and into the Main Plaza. Ramon Alcaraz recalled that Monterrey looked like a "great cemetery" filled with "unburied corpses and…dead animals," the bodies in the streets creating a "terrifying scene."[53] (Ramon Alcaraz was a Mexican officer who wrote many books about the Mexican-American War.) The Mexican troops abandoned their positions and retreated into the city's sizeable central cathedral. Large groups of civilians had sought refuge near the cathedral, which housed a substantial store of ammunition. The Americans advanced within two blocks of Monterrey's Main Plaza before General Taylor ordered a withdrawal.

As the day broke on September 24, after spending the night caring for their horses, Hays led his men back to the city's outskirts and rejoined the fight. The Rangers felt that the enemy was now in their grasp. At last, the old score of Mier was about to be settled. However, much to the Texans' displeasure, an hour-and-a-half truce negotiated by Colonel

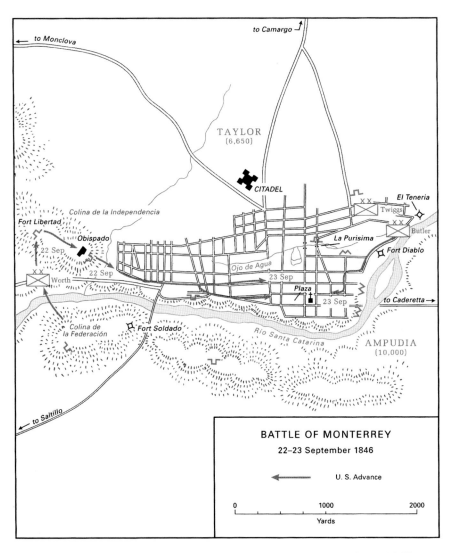

Map of Battle of Monterrey, September 22–23, 1846. *Courtesy U.S. Army Center of Military History, CMH Pub. 73-1.*

Jefferson Davis and Colonel Albert Sidney Johnston was declared. During the truce period, both armies used the time to improve their positions. The Texans went to work with axes and bowie knives, picking holes through the rooftop parapet walls so they could fire from a prone position at the Mexicans. Then, General Taylor extended the cease-fire, and at 5:00 p.m., he announced a truce. The battle for Monterrey was over. With no avenue of escape, General Ampudia surrendered.

The Siege of Monterrey Third Day. Lithograph by Sarony & Major. *Library of Congress.*

Battle of Monterrey. Americans forced their way to the Main Plaza on September 23, 1846. Lithograph by N. Currier. *Library of Congress.*

Capitulation of Monterrey. General Ampudia was treating capitulation on September 24, 1846. Lithograph by Sorony & Major. *Library of Congress.*

The Americans lost 120 killed, 368 wounded, and 41 missing. Officially, the Mexicans recorded their losses as 367 killed and injured. Texas Rangers in Hays's First Texas Regiment in General Worth's division suffered 8 killed, including Captain Ad Gillespie, and 17 wounded. Colonel Wood's Second Texas Regiment in General Butler's division sustained 2 dead and 4 wounded. When a Mexican truce team approached a group of Texas Rangers, Lieutenant William "Big Foot" Wallace aimed his gun at a Mexican officer carrying a white flag. Wallace marched over to the Mexican officer and demanded to know if he would like to hold a bean lottery. (Wallace was one of the Texan prisoners captured in the Mier Expedition in December 1842 who had to draw beans, a black bean meaning death.) Wallace held up his hand without giving the man time to answer. "Look at that hand. Do you know it? Ever see it before?" When the Mexican said he hadn't, Wallace fumed, "Yes, you did, and called up others to look at it." Wallace remembered that the Mexican officer hung his head "like a coyote."[54]

Hays's Ranger captains were outraged that the fighting had stopped. But General Taylor had had enough. The capitulation, of course, disappointed the Rangers' long-cherished hopes of vengeance.[55] The Rangers came to fight, not parley, and they thought that victory had been snatched from their grasp again by the cunning Mexicans. Big Foot Wallace stated, "Whenever [the Mexicans] hoisted the white flag and succeeded in persuading the Americans to 'parley,' they invariably got the better of them in one way or other."[56] But worse, Taylor had offered very generous surrender terms. Ampudia's men were allowed to leave the city with 21 rounds of ammunition, their cavalry horses, and a battery of field artillery. Even more shocking to the Texans, Ampudia agreed to retire beyond Rinconda Pass, and in return, Taylor agreed not to advance past Monterrey for eight weeks.[57] The Texans considered the surrender terms folly. The Texans knew that someone would have to fight these Mexican troops again. They were right. Santa Anna was determined to build an invincible army. Already leading 3,000 men, Santa Anna ordered General Ampudia and his 4,000 remaining soldiers to join him.

Jack Hays led his angry, disappointed Rangers back to camp. They were grateful for a night's sleep and for their tobacco-chewing friends who dressed their wounds with fresh chews.[58] Although uncontrollable at times, Hays's Rangers were magnificent in the fight for Monterrey. Following Hays's standing order to "Give them hell!" Hays's Rangers smashed enemy cavalry charges and stormed redoubts, rooftops, thick-walled adobe houses, and anywhere the Mexicans took shelter. General Taylor owed Hays and his Texans quite a debt for his victory of Monterrey, but he was not at all that sorry to see them ride home when their six-month enlistment expired. "On the day of battle, I am glad to have Texas soldiers with me, for they are brave and gallant, but I never want to see them before or afterward," General Taylor remarked.[59] Taylor began mustering out the Rangers on the last day of September 1846.

General Taylor thanked Hays and the other officers personally and in his correspondence.[60] General Worth, under whom the Rangers fought, praised Hays's Rangers in his after-action report to Washington, noting, "Every individual in the command unites…in admiration of the distinguished gallantry and conduct of Col. Hays and his noble band."[61] "Hereafter, they and we are brothers," Worth wrote proudly, "and we can desire no better guarantee of success than by their association."[62] General Worth had watched Hays's Rangers fight under various conditions and declared they were the best light troops in the world. Of Hays, Worth often said, "Jack Hays is the tallest man in the saddle in front of the enemy I ever saw."[63] Other Rangers also received high accolades. In his report, General Archibald Henderson paid a high tribute to Captain Ad Gillespie, the first on the ramparts of the foe.[64]

The occupation of Monterrey began, and it would last for two years. Meanwhile, Santa Anna had returned from exile in Cuba to a grand reception in Mexico City and reemerged as president-general of Mexico. Santa Anna departed Mexico City for San Luis Potosi, gathering an army of 20,000, including Ampudia's tattered thousands. Santa Anna marched north to attack and destroy Taylor and his army. He boasted that with superior numbers and with the courage of his men, he would destroy Taylor, reclaim Texas, and sign a peace treaty in Washington.

11

SAVING TAYLOR'S ARMY

Absence of Rangers caused many disasters.

W hen the news of Taylor's victory at Monterrey reached Washington on October 11, 1846, President Polk wrote in his diary: "He [Taylor] had the enemy in his power & should have taken them prisoners...and preserved the advantage he had obtained by pushing on without delay."[65] Secretary of War Marcy instructed Taylor to terminate the armistice immediately.

When General Taylor learned that the government disapproved of the truce, he notified Santa Anna that offensive operations would resume on November 13, 1846. Thus, the armistice had ended. On November 16, Taylor occupied Saltillo, but the war's strategy changed as his army inched forward. The strategy planning in Washington shifted away from Taylor's campaign in Northern Mexico and toward an invasion of Central Mexico. General Winfield Scott, General in Chief of U.S. forces, began peeling off Taylor's troops for his amphibious assault on Veracruz. With most of Taylor's regulars leaving to join Scott, Taylor's remaining force now comprised only 4,739 men, and 4,000 were untrained volunteers.

Meanwhile, the crowd-pleasing but ever-erratic Santa Anna continued assembling his army. General Taylor needed good intelligence on the location of Santa Anna's army. Not only did he need to locate Santa Anna's forces, but the absence of Texans to serve as scouts and guides and to carry messages had also resulted in many disasters, including couriers killed, dispatches intercepted, and reconnoitering parties cut off and captured.[66] One of these disasters occurred when Lieutenant John A. Richey, carrying General Scott's orders to Taylor, was set upon by Mexican vaqueros, lassoed and put to a brutal death. Scott's orders confirmed for Santa Anna that Taylor had only a skeleton force of less than 5,000. Knowing Taylor's situation, Santa Anna marched his 20,000 soldiers north to annihilate the meager American force. Santa Anna was so confident of a victory over Taylor that he ordered J.V. Minon and his lancers to Palomas Pass, east of Saltillo, so they could fall on the fugitive Americans streaming north. Then he called for guerrillas to help with the slaughter.[67]

As early as November 30, Benjamin McCulloch (now back in Texas) recognized that the war would begin anew. McCulloch recruited another company of Rangers from Gonzales, and with 27 men, he headed back to Monterrey. Arriving there, McCulloch found that Taylor had moved his headquarters forward to Saltillo. When McCulloch arrived at Saltillo on February 4, 1847, he met with General Taylor and again offered their services. Despite Taylor's ill feelings toward the Texas Rangers in general, he was pleased that Benjamin McCulloch had rejoined him.[68] McCulloch proposed that he and his troops serve for six months. General Taylor wanted their enlistment to be for the duration of the war. McCulloch knew Taylor needed his Rangers' specialized and unique expertise, so he held out for the terms they wanted. McCulloch knew that the General was in a tight place and that the enemy had captured all the reconnoitering detachments sent out.[69] Taylor relented. McCulloch's Company Texas Mounted Volunteers (Spies) mustered in for six months.

McCulloch's Rangers could not have arrived at a better time. Taylor's efforts at gathering intelligence were not going well. On January 22, 1847, another American reconnaissance force, about 70 men, was surprised by 500 Mexican lancers and captured. Then on January 29, 1847, another patrol of Kentucky Volunteers was captured. On February 5, General Taylor advanced his force 17 miles south of Saltillo to Agua Nueva, uncertain of Santa Anna's exact whereabouts. Taylor needed to restore confidence in his green troops. He knew that McCulloch's Rangers' arrival alone could not charge the fighting spirit of Taylor's volunteers, but their knowing how to scout the enemy without being captured, encouraging some.

General Taylor suspected that Santa Anna was moving toward him from the south, and Taylor had no idea how large an army he was facing or even from what direction an attack might come. General Taylor instructed McCulloch and his Rangers to scout the location and strength of Santa

Anna's army, which was believed to be in the mountain pass near the village of Encarnacion. Reports were constantly coming into Taylor that Santa Anna was advancing with 20,000 men, and Taylor needed to know if it was true.

Outside the town of Encarnacion, with 16 hand-picked Rangers, McCulloch captured a Mexican picket, but the Mexican denied that he was part of Santa Anna's army. Riding on and approaching the town that night, they alerted another picket, who fled. When they were about 400 yards from town, the Rangers encountered a line of Mexican cavalry. *"Quien vive?"* broke the silence, then the Mexicans opened fire. Six of McCulloch's Rangers charged the Mexicans. With some mighty yells and the discharge of pistols in the Mexicans' faces, the Rangers put the Mexicans to flight. That was enough for McCulloch. He retired to render his report to General Taylor, having orders not to fight. Walter Prescott Webb adds, "The Rangers returned to headquarters before the day, having triumphed where others had repeatedly failed."[70] McCulloch reported that he believed the enemy he had skirmished with was part of a larger Mexican force. McCulloch won Taylor's approval to again scout toward Encarnacion. But this time, General Taylor sent with the Rangers a large reconnaissance force commanded by Lieutenant Colonel Charles A. May consisting of May's Dragoons, some 400 men, and two artillery pieces.

On the afternoon of February 20, 1847, May's Dragoon force and McCulloch and five hand-picked men—Lieutenant Fielding Alston, a Ranger sergeant, and three Ranger privates—with a volunteer lieutenant from the Kentucky Volunteers joining them, set out to find Santa Anna. Five or six miles from Encarnacion, the two groups parted ways. May's Dragoons went east to reconnoiter around Agua Nueva. McCulloch's Rangers turned south to investigate Encarnacion. At Encarnacion, the Rangers found a Mexican deserter who claimed that Santa Anna was at Encarnacion with his army of 20,000 men. The prisoner was sent on to Taylor's headquarters. Then McCulloch and his men went to see for themselves.

On the night of February 20, McCulloch and his men rode in the dark, slipping through the Mexican

Captain McCulloch interrogates a Mexican prisoner. *Courtesy U.S History Images.*

pickets. About five miles from Encarnacion, reining his horse, McCulloch took in the awesome sight in front of him. Through the clear mountain air he could see hundreds of campfires twinkling in the distance. Santa Anna's Mexican army was indeed there. McCulloch sent Lieutenant Fielding Alston and the others back to report to General Taylor. Then McCulloch, with one other man, Ranger William I. Phillips, slipped closer to the enemy camp to wait and see what daylight would reveal. After climbing a hill, McCulloch and Phillips settled in to await the dawn.[71] They were near enough to see lances gleaming in the light of soldiers' cigars. During the night, they had to play a cat-and-mouse game with a Mexican cavalry patrol that took all the Rangers' skills to avoid being discovered, causing McCulloch and Phillips to spend a cold, sleepless night. When dawn broke, it revealed the Mexican camp in the distance and Mexican pickets building a fire at the foot of the hill not 80 yards from the Rangers. The two Rangers figured that the Mexican camp was nearly a mile long and a fourth of a mile wide. Waking Mexican soldiers began lighting their warming fires. Soon the smoke from the green wood they used blanketed the camp, obscuring the Rangers' view. McCulloch had seen enough. McCulloch and his fellow Ranger departed. Trying to avoid discovery, they rode up on a picket of 20 Mexican soldiers. The two Rangers brazenly pretended to be Mexican mustangers. McCulloch and Phillips slowly rode through the enemy position and safely returned to Agua Nueva. There, they found that General Taylor had decamped and moved on after being warned by McCulloch's returning patrol. McCulloch grabbed some much-needed sleep. Then he headed to Buena Vista. After hearing McCulloch's report, Taylor said, "I am glad they did not catch you."[72]

The information discovered by McCulloch and brought by Alston's squad had caused Taylor to withdraw to a more defensible position, one that could not be flanked or turned. General Taylor had pulled his American force back to Buena Vista on high ground behind a pass that Santa Anna had to bring his force through. Taylor not only had avoided a surprise attack but also was now deployed on better ground. But he still had problems with the quality of his force, mainly being green volunteers. As Taylor waited for Santa Anna's approach, he placed his regular cavalry in reserve behind his thin line of infantry. General John E. Wool was in charge of setting the field of battle. He placed Captain John M. Washington's battery across the road. He then formed a defensive position that included First Illinois under Colonel John J. Hardin, Second Kentucky under Colonel William R. McKee, Second Illinois under Colonel William H. Bissell, and General Joseph Lane's Indiana

Battle of Buena Vista Forces Gathering at Buena Vista, by Henry R. Robinson. *Mexican-American War, Wikimedia Commons.*

Brigade. On the left were Colonel Archibald Yell's Arkansas Volunteers and Colonel Humphrey Marshall's Kentucky Volunteers. Those volunteer horsemen were considered the weak link in Taylor's force. "They were worse than useless and a perfect nuisance," observed Samuel Chamberlain of the U.S. First Dragoons.[73] Two companies of Texas volunteers were at the Battle of Buena Vista. Captain Patrick Edward Conner, held in reserve, commanded one company; the other was Captain Benjamin McCulloch's spy company.

On February 22, 1847, a small party of Rangers found an advance guard of Santa Anna's army. The Rangers quickly withdrew to notify General Taylor at Buena Vista of Santa Anna's approach. Meanwhile, Taylor waited for the arrival of the enemy. Santa Anna's force, reduced to about 15,000 soldiers after surviving the grueling desert march, still outnumbered General Taylor's by more than three to one. A handful of raw, undisciplined militia was about to meet veterans of a regular and thoroughly disciplined army trained for war. It was such a prospect of victory that exhilarated Santa Anna.

On his arrival at Buena Vista, Santa Anna courteously offered Taylor the opportunity to surrender and avoid "catastrophe," but the American commander declined.[74] Santa Anna then ordered the attack on Taylor's

Left: General Santa Anna. Unknown artist. *Mexican-American War, Wikimedia Commons.*

Below: *Battle of Buena Vista*. Lithograph by Adolphe Jean-Baptiste Bayot after a drawing by Carl Nebel. *Battle of Buena Vista, Wikimedia Commons.*

army. The battle was waged for two days and was the bloodiest and most desperately fought engagement of the war, as the Americans repelled assaulting Mexican infantry and lancers. As in the first battles of the Mexican-American War, the American six-pound "flying" artillery batteries played a critical role in the clash. In the two days of fighting, the American artillery repeatedly blunted the Mexicans' attacks, and General Taylor steadied the wavering ranks of his green volunteers.

McCulloch's Rangers took part in the battle, but their small numbers made a minimal impact. The significant contribution of the Texans in the Battle of Buena Vista came earlier in locating the enemy and giving General Taylor the time to deploy for battle. When the battle began at about 8:00 a.m. on February 23, 1847, McCulloch and his Rangers were on the American right flank. The action on the right flank was hot, and the Rangers fought with their usual coolness and skill. McCulloch chased down and captured a Mexican lancer in front of the enemy line. Captain Conner's Texas Volunteers fought alongside the U.S. Second Illinois Regiment. When the smoke of battle cleared, Taylor's army rejoiced; the Mexican army was gone. With 267 soldiers killed and 468 wounded, Buena Vista had claimed more American casualties than any other battle in the war, but Santa Anna's army lost some 1,500 killed and wounded.[75] After the battle, McCulloch and Major Andrew Jackson Coffee toasted victory with a bottle of the major's champagne. McCulloch pronounced it the best wine he had ever tasted.

Fortunately for General Taylor and the Americans, McCulloch was in the field with his Rangers. Thanks to McCulloch's reconnaissance, Taylor's army not only escaped a surprise assault by Santa Anna's forces but also had time to choose its fighting ground and deal out a decisive victory. The Rangers had found Santa Anna's army, infiltrated its lines, and returned with the information that directly contributed to the survival of the American army. Had Santa Anna surprised Taylor's army and defeated Taylor, he could have possibly marched on into Texas and made a reconquest of Texas. Instead, Taylor's victory was a devastating blow to Santa Anna.

After fighting at Buena Vista, McCulloch requested leave. He departed on March 5, 1847, leaving the command of the Ranger company to Lieutenant Alston. McCulloch's Rangers remained in Mexico until late May when they mustered out of service at the end of their six-month enlistment.

IV

LOS DIABLOS TEJANOS

12

UNWASHED, UNKEMPT HELLIONS

Cry vengeance for Texas.

"Old Rough and Ready," General Zachary Taylor, acknowledged that the Rangers' contribution to the U.S. war effort was vital. However, the Rangers' unruly behavior was evident from the time they arrived at Reynosa. "Reynosa, from its history, population, and reputation, was the most rascally place in all Mexico," wrote Samuel C. Reid Jr., serving with McCulloch's Rangers. "The inhabitants are a set of the most irreclaimable scoundrels to be found anywhere in the valley of the Rio Grande—a race of brigands, whose vowed occupation is rapine and murder. It was here that the Mier prisoners were treated so inhumanly as they were marched through on their way to the Castle of Perote, the men cursing and stoning them as they moved through the streets, and the women were spitting on them with all malice of she-wolves. It was this place, too, that many of the robbing parties, which ravaged the Texas frontier acknowledged as their headquarters."[76] Using Reynosa as a forward base to reconnoiter routes to Monterrey, a company of Texas Rangers occupied it during the July 4 holiday. During the celebration, they consumed two horse troughs of whiskey and many local chickens and hogs that "died accidentally." Then General Taylor moved his forces to Camargo. After scouting the region, McCulloch's Rangers arrived at Camargo on July 9, 1846. It turned out that the Rangers had spent much of their scouting time looting liquor and food from farmers and villagers. Samuel Reid admitted that orders were most strict not to molest any unarmed Mexican, but if some of the most notorious villains were found shot or hung up in the chaparral, "*Quien sabe?*"[77]

The Rangers' unruly behavior underscored the difficulties of controlling an irregular volunteer force. These men volunteered to fight, but they were undisciplined and caused problems. The violent and conflicted past instilled many former Texas Rangers, and other Texas volunteers, with hatred and prejudice against Mexicans. Many of the Rangers were former prisoners of the Mier expedition. For these individuals, the United States' declaration of war on Mexico was an opportunity to avenge past suffering and deaths perpetrated by Mexicans. Nowhere is this better exemplified than in the words of a famous Ranger song: "Spur! Spur in the chase, dash on to the fight—Cry vengeance for Texas! And God speeds the right."[78] The Rangers were motivated more than any allegiance to the cause of the United States. As a result, many Mexican War diaries and memoirs give firsthand descriptions of the Rangers' participation and unruly behavior in the conflict.

13

COLLECTING PAST DEBTS

They were men who took an eye for an eye.

In the desolate wilderness of Northern Mexico, free from army discipline, Rangers avenged past and present injustices on their terms, mixing their personal goals with those of the United States Army. Although driven by a desire to collect on "past debts," General Worth, who led the Texans, seemed little concerned about reports of crimes against Mexican civilians. Many Texans viewed the war as a means of exacting revenge on Mexico and the Mexican people, and Texans fought to redress past wrongs and settle old scores. Texas Ranger "Buck" Barry, whose three-month term of enlistment expired before Monterrey's battle, said, "Some of us had traveled 600 miles to kill a Mexican and refused to accept discharge until we got to Monterrey where a fight was waiting for our arrival."[79]

The Texans considered Monterrey a city that was theirs to plunder. Regimental Adjutant John Salmon Ford later recalled: "When the Rangers arrived, many Americans were being killed within the city, but now men had come who took an eye for an eye, tooth for a tooth....This action had much influence in shaping subsequent events, for whilst it greatly elated the American forces, it produced corresponding depression on the Mexicans."[80] One regular army officer later estimated that Jack Hays's men, running roughshod in the city after the battle, killed as many as 100 residents, burned the thatched-roof jacales of peasants, and committed other atrocities.[81] These instances did not involve the whole command, yet all Texans were painted with the same brush.

After the capture of Monterrey, the Texas-mounted riflemen emerged as a liability for General Taylor in the next phase of the conflict: occupation. In addition to the army no longer requiring their forward reconnaissance services, the volunteers' discipline and brutality toward Mexican civilians had become a liability for stability operations. As their excesses threatened to rouse the Indigenous people, Taylor complained that the mounted men of Texas had scarcely made one expedition without unwarrantedly killing a Mexican. Some individuals' criminal actions tarnished the Texas Rangers' reputation and besmirched their hard-won battlefield accolades. Rather than deal with the problem, Taylor merely wished it away by discharging the two Texas regiments, Hays's First Texas Regiment and Wood's Second Texas Regiment, on September 30, 1846. "With their departure, we may look to a restoration of quiet and order in Monterrey," Taylor informed the adjutant general of the army on October 6, "for I regret to report that some shameful atrocities had been perpetrated by them since the capitulation of the town."[82]

If Taylor could rejoice over the seizure of Monterrey, he could not solve the recurring problems of the behavior of his troops. A decade of warfare with the Mexicans made the Texans antagonistic. But the Texans were not the only ones causing problems. On October 5, 1846, a Mexican lancer riding down one of Monterrey's streets was shot without provocation by a regular American soldier. Since no American law applied, all Taylor could do was discharge the man and send him home. It was the same for the volunteers. General Taylor's dismissal of the Texas Mounted Volunteers made it clear his disapproval of the Texans' brutal methods and mercenary motives. He might have disliked their lawlessness and methods, but he still needed the Texans' skills and used them for his most dangerous and dirty tasks. They were indispensable in combat and intolerable in peace. Before the Texas regiments left Monterrey, Taylor requested that Benjamin McCulloch return, with another spy company, if hostilities resumed.

Having been discharged after the Battle of Monterrey, while Hays's Rangers were returning to Texas, two Comanches stampeded the horses except for McCulloch's and another Ranger's. The two men pursued the raiding Indians, dodging arrows until one struck McCulloch's horse, forcing him to dismount. They wounded one of the Indians, and the other fled, leaving the Rangers' horses behind. After returning to Texas, Hays and Walker traveled to New Orleans, where they received a hero's welcome. Walker returned to his native Maryland, and Hays returned to Texas. Samuel Walker, who became a captain of the U.S. Regiment of Mounted

Riflemen, was sent to Washington to lobby for an improved revolver for the mounted troops.

In October 1846, Walker became involved with Samuel Colt by suggesting improvements to the five-shot Paterson Colt that the Rangers used so effectively.[83] Walker told Samuel Colt that if he could "beef up" the five-shot revolver, it might be the weapon to beat Santa Anna and end the war. Samuel Walker and Samuel Colt worked out the specifications for a new pistol. Virtually a hand cannon, the new weapon weighed four pounds, nine ounces. Its six chambers held conical .44-caliber bullets weighing 220 grains with 50 grains of black powder. It was formally designated the "Walker" model. The weapon was as deadly as a rifle up to 100 yards and better than a musket out to 200 yards. The "Walker Colt" pistol was issued during the Mexican War and gave the Americans and Texans an edge in later fighting. Convinced that there was no shelter from this new weapon, Mexicans felt defeated when they went into battle.[84]

14

RANGERS BRANDED THE WORST

No more troops from Texas.

In many cases, regular U.S. Army officers criticized the Rangers' actions mostly based only on rumors and without firsthand knowledge and branded the Texas Rangers "the worst offenders."[85] General Taylor was one of them. On June 2, 1847, Taylor wrote to the Adjutant General: "I deeply regret to report that many of the twelve-month volunteers in their route hence of the lower Rio Grande, have committed extensive depredations and outrages upon the peaceful inhabitants. There is scarcely a form of crime that has not been reported to me as committed by them, but they have passed beyond my reach, and even were they here, it would be next to impossible to detect the individuals who thus disgrace their colors and their country. Where it was possible to rouse the Mexican people to resistance, no more effectual plan could be devised than the one pursued by some of our volunteer regiments now about to be discharged. So far, the volunteers for the war give an earnest better conduct, except for the companies of Texas horse. I have had little or no complaint of the infantry, but the mounted men from Texas have scarcely made one expedition without unwarrantably killing a Mexican....The constant recurrence of such atrocities, which I have been reluctant to report to the department, is my motive for requesting that no more troops may be sent to this column from the State of Texas."[86]

General Taylor wrote his letter in June 1847, after Monterrey and Buena Vista. Hays's First Texas Regiment and Wood's Second Texas Regiment departed Monterey in October 1846. McCulloch's Rangers remained in Mexico, even after his departure on March 5, 1847, but General Taylor refers to "twelve months'" volunteers. McCulloch's Rangers enlisted for only six months. Taylor refers explicitly to "companies of Texas horse," which is quite likely a reference to other units and other separate Texas-mounted companies operating during the later counter-guerrilla phase of the war. However, in the last sentence, Taylor defiantly stated no more troops from Texas, yet he kept every unit from Texas in his service until their terms of enlistment expired.

The war was costly for both sides. It cost combatants much blood and Mexican inhabitants' lives, and property was lost, leaving an indelible mark on both Taylor's and the Rangers' reputations. Yet the Rangers accomplished what other units in the American army could not. In addition to their invaluable intelligence gathering and their fury in battle, they checked and finally ended the attacks of Mexican guerrillas and irregulars on Taylor's supply lines. There were many opinions about the Texas Rangers' service in the Mexican-American War. "The volunteers have killed five or six innocent people walking in the streets for no other object than their amusement," Lieutenant George Gordon Meade had complained. "They rob and steal the cattle and corn of the poor farmers and act more like a body of hostile Indians than civilized whites."[87] A regular army surgeon wrote home about eight Texans who rode up to a Mexican ranch and started stealing pigs and chickens. The owner came out of his house with his small son to protest, and the Texans shot them both, then killed two servants. They were not punished. Taylor had already given up, feeling that the volunteers were no good and he had no power to curb them. "But, my dear Sir," General Winfield Scott told the U.S. Secretary of War when he learned what was happening, "this is no way to win minds and feelings."[88]

The invasion of Mexico by the United States led to two years of chaos in the northeastern part of the country. Nearly all the small towns from Matamoros to Mier to Saltillo were destroyed. Among those doing the damage were various state volunteer units and discharged volunteers who left a wasteland of ashes and uncountable individual and family tragedies. Swept by war fever, state volunteers eagerly joined Taylor's army in Northern Mexico. Many were vehement racists and vocal proponents of Manifest Destiny, and all were men eager to fight and kill Mexicans. Life in the field and the character and temper of these state volunteers contributed to the barbarity of the war.

At the same time, during the campaigns of 1846 and 1847 in Northern Mexico, roaming gangs of Mexican banditti and guerrillas raided ranchos. They ransacked villages, pillaging the properties of peasants and landlords alike. Their misdeeds were sometimes wrongfully assigned to the *Los malvados Tejanos* ("the evil Texans").[89] Rangers used harsh methods to obtain information about Mexican troops' disposition, location, and strength in arms. The Texans, like their enemies, sometimes pistol-whipped prisoners to extract vital information. They might even loop a rope over the prisoner's neck and hoist him off the ground to improve his memory or drag him through the cactus until he agreed to talk.[90] Rangers were often in conflict with civilian noncombatants. Private Alexander Lander, Galveston Rifles (a part of the First Regiment of Texas Infantry), describes how they lived off the land. "We had several skirmishes with rancheros where we stopped," he recalled. "We were Texans and would help ourselves…to the beef, poultry, and other eatables.…They sometimes tried to prevent us from taking what we wanted or tried to compel us to pay more than it was worth. We killed about fifteen rancheros during the campaign in northern Mexico," he casually recorded.[91]

In another incident, as told by Samuel Chamberlain, sometime in 1847, a company of Rangers roared into Hacienda del Patos in the foothills north of Buena Vista. The Texans were bent on having a good time at the expense of the local villagers. They tumbled into a cantina and imbibed a large amount of liquid spirits. Upon departing hours later, they left behind a lone comrade who had enjoyed too much mescal. Finally realizing that the others had left, the drunken Texan mounted up. Screaming insults and firing his pistol wildly into the air, he spurred his horse across the open courtyard toward the town chapel. There, he brashly galloped into the church sanctuary. He lassoed a large wooden cross and dragged the religious relic into the plaza with a gray-haired priest pleading with the Texan to untie the precious statue. The priest was knocked down and trampled beneath the horse's hooves. Within moments a crowd cried, *"Que mueren los Tejano diablo"* ("die, Texan devil"). Several angry villagers pulled the offending Texan from his saddle. Then the villagers began kicking and beating him. The enraged mob stripped the Texan and tied him to a post. The villagers then skinned him alive with rawhide whips, and afterward, they hung his limp frame on a giant cross that rose above the town plaza.

Before sunset that day, the Texas volunteers returned for their lost companion. What they found caused them to yell with horror. The Rangers charged the crowd of Mexicans. They spared neither age nor sex, using their revolvers and bowie knives in their fury, and before long, bodies of slain men and women littered the courtyard.

It was then that the Rangers discovered that the subject of their revenge was still alive but in "awful agony." As the blood-splattered Rangers cut him down, the young man was said to have begged his friends to end his suffering. "Finding him beyond hope," Samuel Chamberlain recorded, "the Ranger captain put a bullet through the brain of the wretch."[92] The news of the incident reached General John E. Wool, but according to Chamberlain, the army kept the matter quiet for its reputation.

A surgeon with General Taylor's division, S. Compton Smith, illustrated Rangers' animosity toward Mexicans in his description of a Texas volunteer named Connelly. According to Smith, this soldier had lost three brothers, all killed before the war by Mexicans in Texas. Smith stated, "Connelly's hatred towards the entire Mexican people was intense, and this hate led him to enlist as an opportunity to avenge his murdered brethren."[93] His opportunity occurred while Connelly defended an army supply train attacked in early March 1847. So intense was Connelly's hatred that he ran headlong into a company of lancers and managed to kill two or three before the Mexicans stopped him. Smith does not mention Connelly's status as a Texas Ranger, and Texan volunteer does not necessarily signify Texas Ranger. However, Connelly's extreme behavior exemplified the contempt that some Texas volunteers, including Rangers, held for Mexicans; this incident also proves that many participated in the war to avenge their troubled and violent history with Mexicans.

The character of the Texas Rangers was already well known by friends and foes. As a mounted soldier, the Texas Ranger had no counterpart in any age or country; he was un-uniformed and undrilled. He performed his active duties thoroughly but with little regard for order or system.[94] General Taylor's letters contain several references to the behavior and attitudes of the Rangers as the most daring of fighting men in all of Mexico. Taylor believed that if the Texans could be subordinated, they would be among the best volunteer units under his command. But he concluded they were too licentious to do much good. Despite his reservations, Taylor readily accepted the services of the Rangers throughout his campaign. They were willing and able to do what his regular cavalry could not. Yet, when General Taylor's Special Order No. 149 called for the final discharge of the volunteers, it did not mince words: "Get the Rangers out of service."[95]

15

TEXANS ARE NOT THE ONLY ONES

Not all the trouble came from Rangers.

The Texan volunteers undoubtedly caused General Taylor problems. However, incidents did not end with the Rangers' departure. After the Texans were discharged and left, other riotous volunteers took their places. Seventy-five thousand state volunteers had eagerly enlisted in volunteer regiments to serve in Mexico. Some of these volunteers, particularly the Arkansas and Kentucky Volunteers, also took vengeance on the Mexicans. The criminal actions of specific individuals and volunteer units tarnished the reputation of all volunteers from all states.

A group of men of the Kentucky Volunteers broke into a Monterrey residence, threw out the husband, and raped his wife. Soon after that, a Kentuckian was found dead with his throat slashed. In the following days, other persons, Mexican and volunteers, were wounded or killed due to the initial crime. Victims included a 12-year-old Mexican boy who was shot in the leg.[96] The war between Kentucky Volunteers and Mexicans appeared to be the result of extreme atrocities and depredations on the part of both sides. Such incidents created tension that inevitably manifested in numerous vicious acts during the city's occupation.

Samuel Chamberlain, U.S. First Dragoons, told of a story involving Arkansas Volunteers while his company was stationed at Agua Nueva. On Christmas Day, Chamberlain and his comrades prepared an elaborate holiday meal. Just as they were ready to eat, a mounted volunteer rode through the camp, signaling the approach of the Mexican army. Chamberlain's dragoons promptly readied for battle. As they prepared to march, Chamberlain witnessed an unruly mob of volunteers descending on the camp and his precious meal. Now confined to their ranks, the Dragoons watched helplessly as the volunteers consumed their Christmas dinner. Chamberlain bitterly lamented the injustice of being robbed of their dinner by volunteers. However traumatic the circumstances, they maintained order and marched out, only to be met by a gang of "Rackensackers," Arkansas Volunteers. Observing a cloud of dust in the distance, an Arkansas officer claimed to have frightened the enemy into retreat. But the enemy's dust turned out to be a herd of wild mustangs. Cursing all volunteers, Chamberlain and his fellow dragoons returned to camp for a Christmas dinner of hard bread and salt pork.[97]

However amusing the Christmas dinner story was, what the Dragoons witnessed en route to meet the presumed enemy was not. When passing the Agua Nueva Ranch, the regulars found the place overrun by Arkansas Volunteers, who were committing all manner of outrages on the few women left in the ranch. The Arkansas Volunteers were fighting over their poor victims like dogs. Chamberlain and his fellow Dragoons attacked the volunteers with swords and drove them away. The Dragoons resumed their march, finding only the herd of mustangs. This was only one account in a long series of atrocious acts committed by volunteers from Arkansas. Chamberlain had accompanied the Central Division, also known as the Army of Chihuahua (even though they never reached Chihuahua), marching from San Antonio to Saltillo, Mexico. Throughout the journey, Chamberlain was often absent from the main army due to his duties as a forager, dispatcher, and scout. But he spent enough time with the Rackensackers to confirm their notorious reputation. Ten companies formed the Arkansas Volunteers. Commanded by Colonel Archibald Yell, Yell's companies were notorious for their unruly behavior. General John E. Wool, commander of the Central Division, contemptuously referred to them on occasion as Colonel Yell's Mounted Devils.[98] Their blatant insubordination resulted in numerous depredations against Northern Mexico inhabitants.

As for Archibald Yell, he had served as governor and congressman in Arkansas before the war. After his death at the Battle of Buena Vista, a Little Rock newspaper printed a lengthy obituary. The obituary states: "When the news reached Washington that the Mexicans had dared to cross the Rio Grande and spill the blood of our citizens upon their soil, he was among the most active in bringing forward measures...to drive them from our soil and punish their insolence." According to Chamberlain, the Arkansas Volunteers regularly raided local ranches, committing all manner of outrages on the inhabitants. But beyond any other possible reasons for their behavior, the Arkansans appeared to commit atrocities for the same reasons other volunteer units did. In times of need, the Arkansans did not hesitate to steal what they needed from locals. They raped Mexican women, as witnessed by Samuel Chamberlain on Christmas Day 1846. In Chamberlain's opinion, the Arkansas Volunteers viewed the Mexican as belonging to a lower social class. As a result, they plundered and ill-treated them. Yell and his Mounted Devils vigorously prosecuted the war.

The worst atrocity of the Mexican-American War directly involved Arkansas Volunteers. Finding 1 of their men murdered, 100 of Yell's Rackensackers chased some Mexican refugees into a cave, shooting and scalping 20 to 30 of them. General Taylor was so enraged that he had the two companies involved sent north to the Rio Grande as punishment. Because Taylor took so little action in disciplining the outraging volunteers, Mexican public opinion turned against the occupying American forces.

The memoirs of Samuel Chamberlain, *My Confessions: Recollections of a Rogue*, contain the most graphic and detailed descriptions of volunteer excesses. Equally revealing were the recollections of army surgeon S. Compton Smith. In *Chile con Carne: The Camp and the Field*, Smith describes the vicious guerrilla warfare and its effects on American troops, Mexican irregulars, and civilians. The misdeeds of volunteers also appear throughout the correspondence and memoirs of such military leaders as Zachary Taylor, Winfield Scott, Ulysses S. Grant, George B. McClellan, and George G. Meade.

V

ON TO MEXICO CITY

16

A WAR WITHIN A WAR

A guerrilla war.

The war in Northern Mexico did not end with General Taylor's victory at Buena Vista but continued as a dirty guerrilla war along his extended supply lines. The American occupation force soon learned that combat operations were far from over. The Mexican guerrillas were expert horsemen and heavily armed with rifles, pistols, lances, sabers and daggers. They were masters of the local terrain. They would strike and then disappear into the countryside. As a result, chaos and conflict—not just from the war—engulfed Northern Mexico in 1846. Doubling as patriots and bandits, they had an established role in Mexican military tradition. Many guerrillas failed to differentiate between their victims and often attacked fellow citizens for personal gain. Their victims were just as often Mexican citizens as U.S. soldiers. Mexico also employed irregular cavalry, raised from local ranchers and commanded by regular troops. The Mexican government used these guerrilla and irregular forces to harass the U.S. Army supply lines. General Antonio Canales and General José de Urrea were two leaders.

On February 24, 1847, a massacre occurred of a large supply train of 110 wagons and 300 pack mules loaded with commissary stores and accompanied by two U.S. infantry companies as escorts. About nine miles from Marin, a band of General Urrea's mounted guerrillas attacked the wagon train. Mexican teamsters were lassoed, stripped naked, and dragged through the cactus before being mutilated. A 16-year-old boy driving a forge used to heat metal was lashed in front of the billows and set afire; another teamster had an incision made in his abdomen, cartridges inserted and the victim blown up. After plundering what they wanted, the guerrillas set fire to the train. Three wagons loaded with ammunition blew up, killing many of the Mexican guerrillas. The American escorting guard offered no resistance and cowardly stood by.[99] Colonel Samuel R. Curtis, Third Ohio Regiment, visited the massacre scene and said the bodies were strewn for two or three miles. Curtis realized the dangers of such guerrilla activity along the supply lines. As commander of the American garrison at Camargo, Curtis wrote the Governor of Texas on March 2. He requested 2,000 men for four months, stating that General Taylor was threatened not only by a large Mexican army in his front but also by a considerable guerrilla and irregular force in his rear.

Curtis's letter triggered the entry of a third significant group of Texan volunteers to the northern theater of the Mexican-American War. These units would fight a bitter counter-guerrilla war, and although most would serve nobly, others committed depredations equal to those of their Mexican guerrilla foes. Major Michael Chevallie's Battalion of Texas Mounted Volunteers, three companies strong, responded to the call for help against the Mexican guerrillas and quickly departed San Antonio for Camargo. The battalion was organized in November 1846, shortly after the battle of Monterrey, but had not been called forward into Mexico. Many men and officers who joined the battalion had fought at Monterrey. Also responding to Colonel Curtis's call for immediate assistance was Captain Mabry B. Gray's Texas Mounted Volunteers from Corpus Christi. Although not officially a part of Chevallie's Battalion, Gray's men operated in the same area during the same periods, and therefore their actions and reputations are intertwined.

S. Compton Smith, a surgeon with General Taylor's army, divided the Rangers in the Mexican-American War into two groups, "real Rangers" and "so-called Rangers." He identified the "real Rangers" as the veterans of the northern Mexican campaign. Smith acknowledged their participation in every battle from Palo Alto (May 8, 1846) to Buena Vista (February 22–23, 1847). Many in this group had fought Indians and Mexicans during the nine years of the independent Republic of Texas period. Smith had nothing but praise for these Rangers. But he described another group of "so-called Rangers" or companies of mounted Texans and noted their later entry into Mexico after formal military operations ended. According to Smith, they were mostly made up of adventurers and vagabonds whose whole object was plunder.[100]

One group under the leadership of the infamous Mabry B. Gray (he was known as "Mustang Gray") committed needless violence that prolonged the conflict in Northern Mexico. Colonel Curtis ordered Mustang Gray's unit to convoy escort duty along the road between Monterrey and Camargo. It was a fateful decision. Gray carried a reputation for excess and was known for his brutal treatment of Mexicans. Mexican raiders had slaughtered Gray's entire family in 1840. Gray was accused of the murder of several Mexicans in 1842 near Goliad but was never arrested.[101]

On May 20, 1847, a large supply convoy departed Camargo with an escort that included Mustang Gray's Texans. Major Luther Giddings of the U.S. First Ohio Volunteers, who accompanied the supply train, noted that Captain Gray and his Texans separated from the command for the supposed purpose of obtaining forage. After the supply train column encamped at the stream near Marin for the night, Giddings said he was informed that one of the Texans had recognized a brother among the decaying remains in the valley and, with tears of grief and rage, had insisted on avenging his death in the blood of the first Mexicans they encountered. When Gray's Texans rode out, Giddings said it seemed to bode evil to the neighboring ranchers.[102] The Texans fell on the nearest pueblo, Rancho Guadalupe. They surrounded the place in the middle of the night, rounded up all 24 men found asleep, and shot them. Because the local inhabitants feared reprisal, Mustang Gray again escaped justice.[103]

The Mexican guerrillas' war became a war within a war, especially after April 4, 1847, when Antonio Canales sent an order to Mexican commandants under his control. He called for martial law and declared that any individual capable of bearing arms was to take up arms against the Americans, and if they did not, they were considered traitors and shot. To carry on the counter-guerrilla fight, Taylor still required the Rangers' services, but as new Ranger units arrived, he trusted their leaders less and less. Units like Mustang Gray's Texans further damaged Taylor's opinion of the Texas Rangers.

As the counter-guerrilla war dragged on, American generals tested the new Ranger leadership even though they had notable success. In August 1847, Major Chevallie quarreled with General John E. Wool and resigned his command, and Captain Walter P. Lane succeeded him. On reporting for duty to Taylor's headquarters in Monterrey, Captain Lane received orders to take the Rangers (Chevallie's Battalion of Texas Mounted Volunteers) down to Cerralvo to capture or kill a band of guerrillas under Juan Flores. It was Flores and his men who were suspected of being the actual persons responsible for killing the American teamsters in February. Scouting the area surrounding Cerralvo, Lane's Rangers soon found a guerrilla camp of about 30 and charged them, killing or wounding about 8 or 10. The rest escaped into the chaparral. Before the Rangers left, two Mexicans led the Rangers to a nearby village, where Lane and his men captured Flores. The Rangers held a trial, found Flores guilty, and shot him. Upon reporting his actions to General Taylor, Lane said that General Taylor was well pleased with his mission, stating it would be a death blow to guerrillas in that part of the country.[104]

With reports that General José Urrea was massing troops at the town of Madelina, General Taylor ordered Captain Lane into the interior to confirm the report. Lane had a small force of 300 men, and General Taylor was sending them into a hostile country against Urrea, who reportedly had 10,000 men. Even with apprehension, Lane led his men on the mission. Upon nearing Madelina, Lane issued orders to his men concerning the use of deadly force, the only such order found in the historical records of the Texas Rangers' Mexican war service. Lane wrote that his men were instructed: "If they came across any armed Mexicans, to order their surrender and fire upon them if they refused."[105]

However, some Texans refused to answer to any civil or military discipline during this counter-guerrilla war. The atrocious actions of some individuals were far more severe than any such incidents committed by the average Mexican-American War volunteer or Texas Ranger. According to General Taylor and his staff, one of the most infamous was a protégé of Mustang Gray's named John Glanton, who had a penchant for scalping the enemy. He was a loathsome desperado, a short, stocky, swarthy ruffian with deep sunk eyes that gave him the appearance of a "wild beast." And he had a violent temper. Samuel Chamberlain saw Glanton slash the throat of a young Ranger in a San Antonio cantina in an argument. Chamberlain said of Glanton that he was always hanging around the army without belonging, often going out with scouting parties but always independent of all authority. Glanton was loyal only to himself, as evidenced by his service to the famous Mexican General José Urrea at the war's end.[106]

Reaching Madelina, Captain Lane entered the town. When an armed Mexican galloped toward them, he was ordered to stop, but the Mexican turned and fled. John Glanton pursued the Mexican on a fast horse and quickly overtook him. Glanton ordered the man in Spanish to halt. When the man showed no signs of halting, Glanton shot and killed him, then seized his horse. Lane's Rangers returned to Taylor's headquarters several days later to report. Lane was shocked at General Taylor's demeanor on the command's return. Lane wrote that General Taylor referred to his command as a set of robbers and cutthroats.[107]

The Governor of Madelina sent General Taylor a letter decrying the Rangers' actions. The Governor accused the Rangers of murdering the fleeing man in cold blood, taking provisions and forage without pay, and general bad conduct. When Taylor ordered the arrest of the tomahawk-wielding rogue John Glanton, Lane refused. Captain Lane defended Glanton's actions. Lane persuaded the scalp hunter to escape to Texas to avoid a court-martial and possible execution as a war criminal.[108] When Taylor's Adjutant, Lieutenant Colonel William W.S. Bliss, arrived at the Rangers' camp with orders to arrest Captain Lane, Lane explained his actions at Madelina. Lane sent for Lieutenant Shackelford (one of Taylor's regular officers), who verified Lane's account of the incident. Afterward, when Bliss met with Taylor, Captain Lane was relieved from arrest. Another incident involved Captain Lane and the accusation of Rangers' theft. Captain Lane received orders to hand over several horses to two local Mexicans who accused the Rangers of stealing. The Mexicans were going to General Wool with witnesses about their ownership of the horses found in the Rangers' coral. Accompanying the Mexicans to the corral to identify the horses in question, Lane's men pointed out a horse belonging to one of Lane's Rangers. In response to the two men's attempt to steal his horse (long a capital crime on the frontier), Lane wrote, "I, being averse to any hard feeling or difficulty, whispered to a few of my men to take the Mexicans down to ravine close by and settle the horse question with them; which they did, giving them about one hundred apiece [presumably punches or blows], the Mexicans barely escaping with their lives."[109] This put an end to the Rangers' horse losses.

Campaigns in Mexico. *Courtesy U.S. History Images.*

Major General Scott at Veracruz on March 25, 1847, by Currier & Ives. *Library of Congress.*

The Rangers' constant vigilance, pursuit, and punishment of Mexican guerrillas resulted in a sharp decline in the number of ambushing guerrilla attacks. On November 7, 1847, Taylor declared the line between Camargo and Monterrey free of hostile parties.[110] Lane's battalion was kept in constant service against Mexican guerrillas until its discharge on June 30, 1848. However, a pronounced shift in American strategy in the war with Mexico occurred in 1847. Major General Winfield Scott prepared for the third campaign into Mexican territory. The first two campaigns in Mexico launched concurrently were Taylor's campaign in Northern Mexico and Brigadier General Stephen W. Kearny crossing mountains and deserts to California, capturing Santa Fe, and securing portions of California.

On March 9, 1847, Scott landed 12,000 regulars at Veracruz in the first large-scale amphibious assault by U.S. military forces. The city was occupied after a 20-day siege.

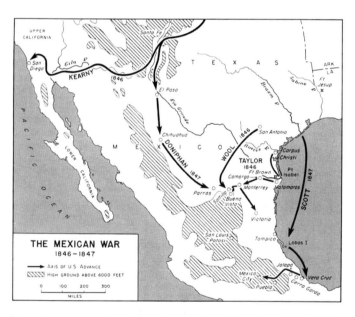

Map of campaigns, Mexican-American War, 1846–47. *Courtesy of U.S. Army. American History Series, AMH-08.*

17

SERVICES NEEDED AGAIN

Rangers needed to solve problems caused by guerrillas.

Although the Mexicans could not check General Scott's progress toward the capital at Mexico City, what they could do was invoke guerrilla warfare on his supply line. The Mexican guerrillas plundered Scott's supply line, cut it, and killed isolated American parties whenever found. Scott's most significant challenge wasn't fighting battles. It was keeping his army supplied. The National Road over which supply trains had to travel wound its way 250 miles from Veracruz in the tropics to La Hoya and Las Vigas, across the Sierra Madre Mountains to Perote, through the great central plateau of Mexico to Puebla and north to Mexico City. Guerrillas infested the entire length of the National Road, and only heavily guarded trains could get through.

Attacks on U.S. Army supply trains increased steadily. Into this situation came Samuel Walker once again. Walker left New Orleans by ship for Veracruz to join General Scott. Though he now held a commission as captain in the U.S. Regular Army, Walker was still considered a Texas Ranger and his men Rangers. He remained a Ranger in tactics and methods. Walker and his 185 men, combined with General Joseph Lane's force of about 3.300, were charged with keeping the supply lines open and stopping guerrilla raids. Of Walker's men, Colonel William S. Harney of the U.S. Second Dragoons observed: "They are all fine, strong, healthy, and

Mexican Guerrillero. Lithograph by N. Currier. *Library of Congress.*

good-looking men. Nearly everyone measured over six feet. So, guerrillas, *robadors* [robbers], take warning for the renowned Captain Samuel H. Walker takes no prisoners."[111]

Now armed with the new six-shot Walker Colt revolvers, Walker's men immediately engaged guerrillas and irregulars at La Hoya and Las Vigas, two towns about 70 miles northwest of Veracruz, killing some 50 Mexicans. Walker and his two companies of mounted riflemen were then assigned to the First Pennsylvania Volunteers and stationed at Castle San Carlos de Perote to counter Mexican guerrillas between Perote and Jalapa. Castle Perote (between the seaport of Veracruz and Mexico City) held a special significance for Walker. The imposing stone walls and the familiar stench of the prison reminded him of the many months of misery he had endured there in the darkness. Walker had vowed to his comrades five years earlier to return one day. The memory of his fellow prisoners' cold-blooded murder haunted Walker. He recalled the infamous "black bean" incident on March 25, 1842, drawing beans to see who would die. Walker remained tormented by the recollections of the mournful cries and moans of dying Texans standing bravely before their executioners. He scribbled in his journal during his imprisonment that he could never forget the embrace of his condemned comrades, and he remembered their last warning to Mexican officers that many other Texans would return someday to avenge them. For Walker, memories of their executions would be more lasting than the massacre of Fannin.[112]

Guerrillas made General Scott's rear a nightmare for him. The wounded or sick on the road or in villages were being murdered. Scott wrote that he feared he could not protect his hospitals established in the larger towns. He discussed the situation with President Polk, who suggested to Secretary of War Marcy that Jack Hays's Texas-mounted regiment be recalled without delay. After returning to Texas, Colonel Jack Hays had directed his attention, once again, to the Indian frontiers of Texas. He stationed the companies of Middleton T. Johnson, Shapley P. Ross, Samuel Highsmith, James S. Gillett, and Henry W. Baylor on the Texas frontier to protect settlers from raiding Indians.

While on the Texas frontier, Hays received an order from the Secretary of War directing him to send whatever portion of his command that could be spared from the Texas frontier to General Taylor and that Hays was to report for duty to Taylor at Monterrey. On August 12, 1847, Hays started for Mier with five companies to join General Taylor again. Meanwhile, General Scott captured and occupied Veracruz on March 29, 1847. As Scott advanced toward Mexico City, Hays received new orders to join

Mier Expedition The Drawing of the Black Bean, by Frederic Remington. *Wikimedia Commons*.

Scott. Hays marched his regiment to Brazos de Santiago, and the first detachment of Hays's men embarked immediately for Veracruz. Hays and the rest of his men reached Veracruz on August 17, 1847, where they drew the first of two consignments of Walker Colt revolvers from the Veracruz depot. While waiting for equipment at the Ranger camp, Hays made several scouting expeditions. A band of 200 guerrillas tried to ambush Hays and 12 men, the Mexicans simply trying to ride over the Texans by sheer weight of numbers. Hays and his Rangers dismounted. With guns aimed across their saddles, they awaited the Mexican onslaught. When the charging Mexican cavalrymen were within 30 yards, a dozen rifles fired. Riderless horses galloped by on either side of the Rangers. Again the Mexicans charged, meeting a rain of lead from six-shooters that emptied more saddles. The Mexican guerrillas withdrew.

Meanwhile, in another engagement with Mexican guerrillas who were causing considerable trouble outside the walls of Veracruz, General Robert Patterson sent Captain John Salmon Ford and his Rangers against Colonel Zenobia, who was particularly troublesome. Colonel Zenobia had a hacienda at San Juan, about 30 miles away. Ford's Rangers marched 25 miles when they came upon the heavily timbered country where parasitical vines obscured the field of vision. Ford was at the head of the column. Seeing a small party of guerrillas ordering a charge, Ford spurred his horse, drew his revolver and dashed off at a gallop. His horse stepped into a small hole in the ground and tumbled over, turning a somersault and sending Ford flying over the animal. Ford, covered in mud, was soon on his feet. This mishap gave the fleeing guerrillas a chance to escape. After a short march, Ford's Rangers advanced on Colonel Zenobia's hacienda. The main building was large and richly furnished with a marble floor. The Rangers found American-made shirts with ball holes in them and blood on them. American corn sacks and many other things were also found. The Rangers told the inhabitants to leave, and then they burned the hacienda. Everything was reported to General Patterson, who said there might be some trouble over burning the house, but nothing came of the matter.

A game of hide-and-seek between Santa Anna and General Joseph Lane's special anti-guerrilla brigade included Walker's Rangers. During two weeks in June 1847, a supply train convoy of nearly 700 foot soldiers and approximately 128 wagons left Veracruz. The supply convoy came under attack three times along its route, fighting through the attacks each time. When the guerrillas were preparing to ambush the column again, Walker's Rangers rushed out of their garrison at Perote and prevented the Mexicans from attacking the supply train. Then, on October 6, 1847, Walker's Rangers and the main body of General Lane's command left Perote for the town of Puebla to lift Santa Anna's siege that the American garrison had endured for weeks. Learning of Lane's approach, Santa Anna pulled 4,000 men from the siege at Puebla and moved them to Huamantla, northeast of Puebla. General Lane received word that Santa Anna was at Huamantla and diverted his column. Lane reached Huamantla on October 9, 1847.

General Lane sent Samuel Walker's Rangers ahead as skirmishers while he followed with infantry. Encountering about 2,000 mounted Mexican lancers outside the town, Walker ordered a charge without waiting for support from the rest of Lane's column marching behind them. The tall cavalier and his men dashed like thunderbolts into the mist of glittering lances of the Mexican cavalrymen, firing their Walker Colt revolvers. With the sudden ferocity of Walker's attack, the Mexican lancers waivered a moment, then broke and fled in confusion into the town.[113] Walker and his men raced into the town. Walker's Rangers were riding through the narrow streets, four abreast, toward the central plaza when musketry started to pop from windows and rooftops. Walker tumbled from the saddle.

A bullet had pierced Walker's lung, and another shattered his skull. (One of the most enduring myths about Walker is that a Mexican lance killed him.) "I am dying, boys," was one version of his final words, "you can do nothing for me now. I'll never see Texas again. Carry me back to San Antonio and bury me with Ad Gillespie."[114] Walker was temporarily buried within a stone wall on the edge of town and eventually moved to San Antonio, where he currently rests. His death left his troopers reeling for safety in a church. The Texans were saved only by Lane's troops reaching the church and relieving the hard-pressed Rangers. With General Lane's infantry on the scene, Santa Anna's Mexican forces retreated farther out of town, effectively ending the battle. The Mexicans withdrew toward Queretaro.

The fight at Huamantla was quick but resulted in 24 American losses and 400 Mexican casualties killed, wounded, and captured. It was a more significant loss for Santa Anna. Within days of his humiliating defeat at Huamantla, the President-General of Mexico was stripped of his command and office. Scott's victorious army had entered the fortress of Mexico City only three weeks before, bringing an effective conclusion to the war with Mexico.

After the fight at Huamantla, General Lane disgracefully told his soldiers to avenge the death of the gallant Walker.[115] Reprisals for the death of Walker

The Death of Captain Walker at Huamantla in Mexico, by Ballie. *Library of Congress.*

came immediately as the Texans swept the town, killing every Mexican they saw. It was a wild rampage, sacking, looting, and pillaging the town. They broke into houses and shops and took whatever they wanted. It was a drunken orgy of violence and destruction. Lieutenant William D. Wilkins described the horrible carnage that followed the victory at Huamantla: "When the men were maddened with liquor, every species of outrage was committed. Older women and girls were stripped of their clothing—and many suffered still greater outrages. Dead horses and men lay about thick while drunken soldiers, yelling and screeching, were breaking open houses and chasing some poor Mexicans." Mexican journalist Ramon Alcaraz confirmed that the Texans already had sown death and fear along the roads from Veracruz and now plundered public buildings and the houses of civilians, murdering those unfortunate ones who resisted immediate surrender of their belongings.[116] General Lane escaped punishment. Santa Anna stepping down as commander of the Mexican Army after the engagement at Huamantla overshadowed the American rampage.

After the capture of Veracruz, General Winfield Scott pushed inland and encountered General Santa Anna's larger army at Cerro Gordo. Scott won a stunning victory after Captain Robert E. Lee discovered a trail that allowed Scott's troops to flank the Mexican position. Pressing on, Scott won

Major General Winfield Scott, General in Chief, U.S. Army, by Currier & Ives. *Library of Congress.*

Major General Winfield Scott Grand Entry City of Mexico. General Scott's grand entry into Mexico City on September 14, 1847, by James A. Ballie, Lithographer. *Library of Congress.*

victories at Contreras and Churubusco on August 20, 1847, before capturing the mills at Molino del Rey on September 8, 1847. At the edge of Mexico City, Scott assaulted Chapultepec, and American forces overwhelmed the defenders and secured the castle. Scott captured Mexico City and made a grand entry on September 14, 1847.

THEY WERE DEVILS INCARNATE

Los Diablos Tejanos! Los Diablos Tejanos!

Hays's Rangers departed Veracruz on November 2, 1847, riding in front of Major General Robert Patterson's volunteer division. Jack Hays's men were the "real Texas Rangers." They wore an outlandish assortment of long-tailed blue coats or bobtailed black ones, slouched felt hats, dirty panamas and black leather caps. Most wore long, bushy beards, their horses were of all sizes and breeds, and each Ranger carried a rifle and four pistols. They also carried short knives, hempen ropes, rawhide riatas, or hair lariats. They carried anything else they chose to tie to their saddles.[117] Hays's Rangers had orders to reopen Scott's supply line and rid the countryside of guerrillas.

General Patterson and Jack Hays's combined force reached Jalapa on November 4, 1847. After arriving there, Hays, with two Ranger companies, pressed on to Puebla, arriving there a few days later. Meeting with Brigadier General Joseph P. Lane, the two men began planning a raid to free Americans who were held captive in nearby Izúcar de Matamoros, south of Puebla. On November 23, 1847, 135 of Hays's Rangers rode on ahead of Lane's column, more than 60 miles in less than 24 hours, through the cold and rain to assault the fortified Mexicans. Hays's attack killed more than 60, including Colonel José Piedras, a Mexican officer well known to Texans as a commander stationed in East Texas in the 1830s. Afterward, Hays's men freed 21 American prisoners and found an arsenal of weapons. The Rangers rejoined Lane's main force. On their way back to Puebla, 200 Mexican lancers attacked the command. Hays immediately moved to the front and ordered a charge that caused the Mexican lancers to turn and flee. Hays's calm leadership again saved the day when the charging Rangers came over a rise and found 500 more Mexican lancers. The Mexicans withdrew when Patterson's flying artillery arrived on the scene. The command returned to Puebla with two killed and two wounded.[118]

Hays's Rangers resumed their army escort duties and arrived in Mexico City on December 6, 1847, at the head of a column of long-overdue replacements for Scott's army. Hays's motley collection of mounted Texas Rangers rode into an already occupied Mexico City. Jack Hays was well known by the Mexican populace as the scourge of the South Texas borderlands. So much so that he had earned in battle the sobriquet *El Diablo* (the Devil).[119] Ford remembered his amusement seeing them attempting to search out the famed ranger commander. Hays was a small man and wore no uniform; some large, good-looking Ranger would often be mistaken for him. Everyone enjoyed the standing camp joke. Of course, no one had the nerve to tell the wiry little commander of such cases of mistaken identity.[120] When Hays rode triumphantly into the Grand Plaza and halted his columns in front of the National Cathedral, a crowd of more than 1,000 pressed forward to get a closer look at the grim-faced Texan. Hays was the object of peculiar interest, as he was the man whose name had been a terror to their nation.[121]

"*Los Diablos Tejanos! Los Diablos Tejanos!*" cried the Mexicans as they crowded along the streets to get a look at the "Texas devils."[122] The frightened onlookers believed the Texans to be a sort of semi-civilized, half man, half devil, a slight mixture of lion and the snapping turtle, and they had a more holy horror of him more than they had of the evil saint himself.[123] Ranger Nelson Lee recollected that the dramatic Texans' entrance resembled a carnival. They were some 900 strong and presented a ridiculous appearance. They were ragged and unwashed, more unkempt than their mounts, and their mounts were a varied assortment of animals ranging from spirited, well-bred geldings and mares to pack mules and long-haired jacks.[124] A correspondent for the *New Orleans Picayune* offered a description of the strange and slow procession, recalling the gallant Rangers riding through the streets. They were covered with mud and dust. The Mexicans were staring at these much-dreaded Tejanos. General Ethan Allen Hitchcock noted the reaction to the mounted volunteers from Texas. "Hays's Rangers have come, their appearance never to be forgotten," he wrote in his diary. "The Mexicans are afraid of them."[125]

That they were "Texas Devils" soon became evident as Hays's Rangers rode through the city. A Mexican street vendor passed by the Rangers with a basket of assorted candies on his head. When one young Texan called him over and reached into the basket to retrieve one fistful of candy and another without offering to pay for the treats, the Mexican became incensed. He picked up a small stone and hurled it at the Ranger; it was the last stone he ever threw. A flash was seen, a report was heard, and the offender fell dead. The Ranger quietly replaced the pistol in his belt and rode on.[126] That single gunshot caused a stampede of men and women, trampling one another in a desperate attempt to escape. The men had come who took an eye for an eye.

Information soon reached General Scott that two Mexicans had been killed as the Rangers entered the city. Having exerted himself to repress all disorder and prevent all outrages, the commanding general dispatched an order for Colonel Hays to appear instantly before him. In five minutes, a gentlemanly young man stood before the Commander-in-Chief of the American army, saluted, and said, "I, Sir, am Colonel Hays, Commander of the Texas Rangers, and report myself to you per an order just received." When Hays came into the general's tent, Scott burst out: "I have been informed, Sir, that since the arrival of your command in this city, two Mexicans have been killed. I hold you responsible, Sir, for the acts of your men. I will not be disgraced, nor shall the army of my country be by such outrages. I require you, Sir, to say whether my information is correct and if so, you will render me a satisfactory explanation." "Your information," replied Hays, "is correct, General." "A Texas Ranger is not in the habit of being insulted without resenting it. They did kill two Mexicans as I entered the city, and I, Sir, am willing to be held responsible for it."[127] The General's wrath began to abate, and after motioning the Colonel to be seated, General Scott requested a full statement of the facts.

As if tensions were not high enough, later that same evening, while several Rangers stood quietly preparing to enter a theater, a mischievous young Mexican, hardly more than a boy, dashed by them and grabbed a bandana from around the neck of one of the Texans. Before the street urchin could run to safety, the offended Ranger leveled his pistol and blew the youngster off his feet, killing him instantly. No sooner had the gunsmoke cleared the air than the Texan walked over, retrieved his bandana, and, according to Adjutant Ford, went on his way as if nothing had happened.[128]

The bloodshed increased sharply on both sides. Major D.H. Hill said, "Five hundred cut-throats from Texas under the command of Colonel Hays entered the city today. These ragged and dirty ruffians murdered and robbed the city's poor. It is said that the Texans have murdered no less than 200 Mexicans since their short residence in the city," Major Hill complained on December 23, 1847. General Scott's volunteers were generally atrocious, but the Texans were hideous, keeping Mexico City in a constant uproar. The trouble peaked when a Texan officer, riding alone through a tough district in Mexico City, was hacked to pieces. The next day, more than 80 bullet-riddled Mexican corpses were found in that section.[129]

Hardly a sunrise passed in the ensuing days without at least one American found dead, either shot or stabbed during the previous night's violence. The city did not take kindly to the American occupation. Soldiers who let their guard down were suddenly stoned or shoved into the gutter. As Adjutant Ford recorded, "Some gringo lost his life every night."[130] One December night, a young man from Captain Jacob Robert's company, Ranger Adam Allsens, foolishly ventured alone into a sordid district of the city known as Cutthroat. Almost predictably, several knife-wielding assassins attacked the young man, stabbing him repeatedly and leaving him for dead. Ford noted that the Texan's chest wounds were so ghastly—one gash supposedly deep enough to reveal his pulsating heart—that even the most battle-hardened soldiers were sickened by the sight of the suffering man. He lived long enough to ask his fellow Rangers to avenge his death. Ford later admitted that such incidents were not reported to U.S. officials. But neither were they forgotten or forgiven by the Rangers, who waited less than 24 hours to settle this particular debt. Ford knew a scheme to wreak a bloody vengeance was afoot.

Hays's men were hell-bent on vengeance, and nothing would stop them. Around ten o'clock the following morning, it was reported to Ford that during the night a unit of regular military police had been dispatched to investigate the disturbance and that they, too, had joined in the indiscriminate shooting. The result was that the bodies of 53 Mexican civilians had already been placed in carts. An updated report raised the estimate to 80 corpses transported in death wagons to a nearby morgue by sundown and then laid out like cordwood. "It was a fearful outburst of revenge," Ford confessed.[131] Several days later, Scott summoned Hays to confront him with the report that Rangers had gunned down six more Mexican civilians in broad daylight. Hays admitted that his men had fired on a group of Mexicans because they were stoning the Rangers as they rode through the streets. "His men had acted in self-defense," Hays insisted. Not wishing to offend an influential friend of President Polk, General Scott asked no further questions, and the matter died there.[132]

General Scott soon found work for highly volatile Rangers outside the capital. Hays's Rangers were sent into the countryside, ostensibly to fight guerrillas but mostly to get them out of the city. The Mexican government recognized and sanctioned any Mexican who would place himself at the head of a company of men to annoy the enemy. For these men, guerrillas, it was an opportunity to commit legalized robbery. They terrorized the Mexican population. For protection, they hid in the mountains, in secure retreats, where they lived with their families. They rode out on their expeditions to raid and plunder from these hideaways, committing all manner of outrages. They enjoyed perfect immunity in their lawless life.

In early January 1848, Jack Hays and about 65 Rangers departed Mexico City to hunt the elusive Padre Jarauta, a notorious guerrilla leader. Led by a Mexican guide, the Rangers marched first to Otumba and then back to Teotihuacán. After finding Teotihuacán nearly empty upon arrival, the Rangers occupied one of the larger buildings on the plaza. Weary from their long march, they went to sleep. Padre Jarauta, with some 1,200 to 1,500 guerrillas, attacked the building where Hays and his men were resting. A sharp conflict ensued. The Rangers reacted quickly. They turned the tables on their attackers, wounding Jarauta and killing 15 or 20 of the enemy while suffering no casualties. Wounded, Jarauta fled, followed by his men.[133]

The Rangers commenced their last counter-guerrilla operation on February 17, 1848. The treaty ending the war was signed on February 2, 1848, but was unratified by Mexico or the United States. So the Rangers continued to fight. "News traveled slowly, and the cooling of blood took longer," wrote Mike Cox.[134] The last Ranger operation of the war was again against Padre Jarauta's band of guerrillas. Having recovered from his wounds, Padre Jarauta continued to fight despite the impending peace. He was reportedly located at Zacualtipan with 450 men. General Lane was determined to make a vigorous effort to exterminate these guerrillas. He planned to pursue them into the mountains, attack them in their strongholds and break them up if possible.

Colonel Hays and General Lane again joined forces to destroy the guerrilla Jarauta. With a force of 250 Rangers and 130 Dragoons, they assaulted Zacualtipan just after daylight on February 25, 1848. In the bitter house-to-house battle that ensued, Jarauta again narrowly escaped. However, the fight effectively destroyed Padre Jarauta's command. As one participant later put it, they had forever "ceased to feast on tortillas."[135] Lane himself accompanied the expedition. He said, "It was a most remarkable sight to see the Rangers run up the mountains in pursuit of the guerrillas, the ease and rapidity with which they ascended the steep and rocky mountainsides, and reached points inaccessible, commanded his hearty admiration."[136] The expedition proved a great success against the guerrillas. The Rangers and Dragoons had destroyed their villages, killed 150 guerrillas, wounded many more, and taken 50 prisoners. Their commands suffered a combined total of five wounded, one mortally. However, afterward, the Texans were berserk. "Zacualtipan, a rich and luxurious town, was sacked and then burned," according to Major Hill. It was Huamantla all over again, leaving about 150 Mexican bodies on the street, mostly civilians. Lane had sent the prisoners to Mexico City, where Hill was the judge advocate of the military court and uncovered the truth of what had happened.[137]

VI

VILLAINS OR HEROES

19

IT WAS A NASTY WAR

The heroism of battle never offsets the horrors of war.

General Scott regarded Colonel Hays and his men as invaluable. His official reports gave them great credit for their active and efficient services in suppressing the guerrillas. Both Taylor and Scott relied heavily on the Texas Rangers throughout the war. They conducted reconnaissance, collected intelligence and carried messages through Mexican lines. The Rangers launched raids against specific targets, especially guerrilla encampments. However, their depredations on the Mexican citizenry were often excessive, and their behavior, along with that of other volunteers, sparked local Mexican resistance. It was a nasty war.

The Rangers left Mexico City on March 18, 1848. Except for Hays and Ford, all Rangers mustered out of federal service on April 29, 1848. They departed for Texas a few days later. The Rangers had ably served as the eyes and ears of General Zachary Taylor's army. "If the Rangers had indulged in excesses, it was because they were an intensely proud band of fighting men who wanted revenge; even if revenge became a cloak for pillage and murder, the Rangers were still honorable men."[138] The Rangers who fought in Mexico returned to Texas as heroes. Although great Rangers like Walker and Gillespie died, most were young men riding off to war. Many who rode roughshod in Mexico would saddle up again as Rangers in Texas, but the attitude of hatred inspired by fighting on both sides of the river would outlive them all.[139]

Warfare brings out the worst in some men but summons the best in others. The Rangers held no monopoly on violence against the Mexican population. Other American volunteer units also caused problems and committed crimes. Wanton acts of violence were committed against the civilian population of Northern Mexico during the campaigns of 1846 and 1847. Roaming gangs of Mexican guerrillas raided ranchos, ransacked villages, and pillaged properties. The guerrillas' misdeeds were sometimes correctly and wrongfully assigned to the evil Texans. Although expected to reinforce the army, the arriving American state volunteers were mobs descending on General Taylor that summer of 1846. These various American volunteer regiments, not just those from Texas, were wildly undisciplined, refused to wear uniforms, caused disorder, squabbled in political disputes, and misused their equipment and arms, draining supplies. The lack of discipline in the volunteer regiments largely explains why such savage behavior occurred. They were eager to fight and kill Mexicans. Not all the atrocities were committed by volunteers and too many discharged volunteers hung around the occupation zone, joined by lowlifes who formed criminal gangs.[140]

And it wasn't only state volunteers who perpetrated atrocities against Mexicans. Brigadier General David E. Twiggs had 16 prisoners whipped until their backs appeared like pounded pieces of raw beef. Branding irons in the shape of the letter D were applied after the whippings to the hips of some and the right cheeks of a few. Other men were hanged. While a battle raged at Chapultepec, not far away, Lieutenant Colonel William S. Harney, with a record as a torturer during the Seminole War, beat some prisoners across the face with his sword. Of the men hanged, one had lost both legs. The whippings were conducted by army corporals with knotted lashes, while nooses were rigged so that the men were strangled to death rather than having their necks broken. Harney's sadistic conduct spread more horror through Mexico City.[141] Huamantla was the only time a general officer, Brigadier General Joseph Lane, permitted his men to sack a town.

Those doing damage during the Mexican-American War, leaving a wasteland of ashes and uncountable individual and family tragedies, included U.S. volunteers, discharged volunteers, guerrillas victimizing civilians, irregulars waging a guerrilla war, and regular military officers, particularly those involved in the counter-guerrilla war. The Rangers' reputations and a history of Texan and Mexican fighting had preceded the Rangers riding into Mexico. The Rangers' fame or infamy spread like a plague through the Mexican population. Villagers in the countryside shuddered in terror on hearing the word of the advance of the *Los sangrientos Tejanos* (the bloody

Texans). Even the most seasoned Mexican lancers learned how frightening the specter of the screaming Rangers was, charging hell for leather into their lines with bullets flying from both fists. Although Ford insisted that his fellow Rangers were, for the most part, men of good character, he admitted that motives of revenge more than a sense of patriotism guided many of Colonel Hays's regiment. "The command had men in it who had suffered the loss of relatives by Mexicans massacring prisoners of war. Some men had been Santa Fe prisoners, Mier prisoners, and prisoners made at San Antonio by Vasquez and Woll. Was it a wonder that it was difficult to restrain these men…who were standing face to face with the people whose troops had committed…such bloody deeds," said Ford.[142] They wanted revenge.

20

THERE WERE HEROES

Walker, McCulloch, Hays, and others.

The first genuine war hero from Texas was Captain Samuel H. Walker, the first to serve with General Taylor. His contemporaries assigned one word more than any other to Walker: *gallant*. Not a large man, he towered in the saddle as he led scouting parties. Whether riding in advance of General Taylor's army or serving as a courier bearing dispatches, he took on the most dangerous reconnaissance missions. He led headlong charges into columns of Mexican lancers. He inspired his men to be as fearless as he was. The memory of Mier and Perote constantly haunted him. He nurtured his loathing for Santa Anna and all Mexicans so much that his friends called him "mad Walker."[143] Samuel Walker came to Texas six years after Texas won its independence but would live for only five more years. During those five years, he defended San Antonio from Mexican forces, invaded Mexico four times, escaped from a Mexican prison, and helped design one of the most famous guns in history, the six-shot Walker Colt. It is said Walker was not someone you would notice in everyday life. He was of average size and quiet. But in battle, he was a lion.[144]

None of General Taylor's scouts during the war proved more resourceful or cunning than Benjamin McCulloch. He bore an appearance that concealed his stealth, courage, and toughness. No one doubted his bravery in battle and his knowledge of fighting, particularly his Indian-style methods of unconventional warfare. Serving under Jack Hays on the Indian frontier in

Left: The gallant Captain Walker of Texas Rangers who fell at the Battle of Huamantla on October 9, 1847, from a daguerreotype by Brady. *Library of Congress.*

Right: Captain Benjamin McCulloch. *Courtesy Samuel C. Reid, Jr.*, The Scouting Expeditions of McCulloch's Texas Rangers, *Philadelphia 1859.*

Texas, McCulloch learned guerrilla-style hit-and-run tactics, the technique of surprising a superior enemy by taking advantage of the terrain, and the importance of doggedly pursuing a demoralized foe in retreat. The word *defeat* was not in McCulloch's vocabulary; neither was patience.[145] McCulloch performed a reconnaissance service for General Taylor that was a critical function in Taylor's victories on the march to Monterrey and the success at Buena Vista. Throughout Taylor's advance into unfamiliar and hostile territory, General Taylor relied on McCulloch's Rangers to enable him to exploit the initiative for his military operations. Their familiarity with the Mexican environment and culture, and their native horses' acclimatized endurance, allowed them to patrol farther than the unprepared U.S. Dragoons. A correspondent once said of McCulloch that he was vigilant as a tiger, a border man, a ranger, and an Indian fighter. Moreover, Benjamin McCulloch was a great man, a backwoodsman, a ruffian, and an unpolished desperado. He was a thinker with a precise and clear mind, not much of a talker. With him, "it is" or "it is not."

Only 30 years of age, a seasoned Ranger leader, already known to the populace as the scourge of the South Texas borderlands, so much so that

John "Jack" Coffee Hays by Mathew B. Brady. *Library of Congress.*

he earned the title *El Diablo* ("the Devil"). He was John Coffee "Jack" Hays. He was no conversationalist and did not appear the least intimidating at first glance. He earned the highest respect from all who served under him. A correspondent of the *New Orleans Delta* in November 1846 said, "Modesty is the most remarkable trait of Colonel Hays, and it is no uncommon thing to hear others characterized as being almost as bashful as Jack Hays." The men who rode with Hays knew him best. There never lived a commander more idolized by his men. His word was law.[146] He did not merely command his men. He led them.

Jack Hays's Texas Rangers acquired and reported intelligence on enemy activities. His men led the U.S. Army through enemy territory, providing a screening flank against enemy cavalry attacks. And there were others like much-respected Robert A. Gillespie (among the casualties of the Battle of Monterrey), Michael Chevallie, John Salmon Ford, and William A.A. "Big Foot" Wallace. The Texas Rangers rode into Mexico in a scheme to wreak bloody vengeance, and nothing could stop them. They were demons on horseback, heroes in battle, and feared by the Mexican people. They rode through the country in vengeance for the Alamo, Goliad, and Mexican atrocities of recent years, continuing an ongoing war. The Rangers were crucial in winning the war, and it is also indisputable that they left a black mark on their reputation. In a turn of history, they were *Los Diablos Tejanos* from the north (rather than Mexican terror from the south). It was a nasty war and a reflection of the times and history between the two countries.

APPENDIX

Texas Mounted Volunteers

General Staff of Texas Volunteers, July 1846 to October 1846. Governor James Pinckney Henderson appointed Major General of combined Texas Volunteer troops at Monterrey.

First Regiment Texas Mounted Rifle Volunteers (Hays's First Texas Regiment) (mostly former Texas Rangers and frontiersmen from the western part of the state), organized in June and July 1846 and discharged in September and October 1846. Commanded by Colonel John C. Hays, serving in Taylor's northern Mexico campaign.

Second Regiment Texas Mounted Rife Volunteers (Wood's Second Texas Regiment), organized in June and July 1846, discharged in October 1846. Commanded by Colonel George T. Wood. The unit was raised in east Texas and served in Taylor's northern Mexico campaign.

Texas Mounted Volunteers, organized by Albert Sidney Johnston, May to August 1846. Served with Generals Taylor and Butler at Monterrey. He was the adjutant U.S. Sixth Infantry and Adjutant General of Texas.

Regiment of Texas Mounted Volunteers for six months (seven companies) from frontier defense, July–September 1846. Commanded by Colonel William C. Young.

A battalion of Texas Mounted Volunteers (four companies), March 1847 to June 1848. Commanded by M.H. Chevallie, who resigned on August 31, 1847, and then commanded by Walter P. Lane to October 1847 in the U.S. Army's campaign against Mexican guerrillas.

Another regiment of Texas Mounted Volunteers raised by Colonel John C. Hays for service with General Scott in his central Mexico campaign. Mustered for twelve months, April 1847 to May 1848.

Independent Companies of Texas Volunteers

First Mounted Company, September 25, 1845, to June 25, 1846 (Captain John T. Price).

Second Company of Rangers, September and December 10, 1845, and March 1846, for two periods of three months each to July 1846 (Captain Peter Hansbrough Bell, who had before served on the frontier defense of Texas, under Major Hays from September 1845).

Third Mounted Company, October 1, 1845, and January 1846 to September 1846 (Captain David C. Cady).

Fourth Mounted Company, May and August 1846 to September 18, 1846 (Captain Ben McCulloch).

Fifth Mounted Company, July to October 1846 (Captain Eli Chandler).

Sixth Mounted Company, July 1846 to July 1847 (Captain Mabry B. Gray, later First Lieutenant in Bell's Company).

Seventh Company of Foot Volunteers (first enrolled in Mississippi), August 1846 to January 7, 1847 (Captain William E. Shivors, later captain in Johnston's Third Rifle Regiment).

Eighth Rifle Company (later Seefeld's Company of Johnston's Third Regiment), September 1, 1846, to July 1, 1847 (Captain P. Edward Connor, later First Lieutenant Seefeld's Company of Johnston's Third Regiment to December 1846).

Ninth J Company Volunteers (at Monterey), October 8, 1846, to October 1847 (Captain Mirabeau B. Lamar, later Division Inspector to Major General Henderson).

Tenth I Company Volunteers, October 1846 to October 1847 (Captain Shapley P. Ross).

Eleventh Mounted Company of Spies, January 31 to July 31, 1847 (Captain Ben McCulloch, major in the staff).

NOTES

Chapter 1

1. Jones, *Memoranda and Official Correspondence*, 604.
2. Clary, *Eagle and Empire*, 67.
3. *London Times*, April 15, 1845, quoted in Smith, *War with Mexico*, 1:105.

Chapter 2

4. Cox, *Texas Rangers*, 100.
5. Moten, *Presidents and Their Generals*, 103.

Chapter 3

6. Urwin, *United States Cavalry*, 77.
7. Moten, *Presidents and Their Generals*, 103.

Chapter 4

8. Taylor to Adjutant General, August 5 and September 1, 1845. *U.S. House Executive Doc 60*, 106.
9. Quotation in Haynes, *Soldiers of Misfortune*, 20.

Chapter 5

10. Greer, *Texas Ranger*, 128.
11. Collin, *Texas Devils*, 12; Webb, *Texas Rangers*, 11; Cox, *Texas Rangers*, 110; Samora, *Gunpowder Justice*, 39.
12. Collins, *Texas Devils*, 9; Jonathan Duff Brown, "Reminiscences of Jon. Duff Brown," *Texas Quarterly State Historical Association* 12 (April 1909): 296; Giddings, *Sketches of the Campaign*, 10; Reid, *Scouting Expeditions of McCulloch's Texas Rangers*, 26.
13. Collins, *Texas Devils*, 9.
14. Collins, *Texas Devils*, 10; Brackett, *General Lane's Brigade*, 173; Hitchcock, *Fifty Years in Camp and Field*, 310.
15. Cutrer, *Ben McCulloch*, 70.

Chapter 6

16. Rickard, *Brief Biographies*, 168; Collins, *Texas Devils*, 8.
17. Webb, *Texas Rangers in the Mexican War*, 8; Cox, *Texas Rangers*, 106.
18. Webb, *Texas Rangers in the Mexican War*, 8; Cox, *Texas Rangers*, 106; Robinson, *Men Who Wear the Star*, 74; Grant, *Memoirs and Selected Letters*, 53; Sowell, *"Big Foot" Wallace*, 122; Clary, *Eagle and Empire*, 143; Dilworth, *March to Monterrey*, 24; Spurlin, *Texas Volunteers*, 20.
19. Webb, *Texas Rangers*, 91; Taylor to Adjutant General, April 15, 1846, *U.S. House Executive Doc 60*, 138; Webb, *Texas Rangers*, 92; Governor J.P. Henderson, April 26, 1846, *Texas Democrat*, May 6, 1846.
20. Robinson, *Men Who Wear the Star*, 74; Collins, *Texas Devils*, 12; Grant, *Memoirs and Selected Letters*, 53.
21. Webb, *Texas Rangers in the Mexican War*, 18
22. Reid, *Scouting Expeditions of McCulloch's Texas Rangers*, 46.
23. Ibid., 51.
24. Webb, *Texas Rangers in the Mexican War*, 28.

Chapter 7

25. *Texas Democrat*, January 27, 1847.
26. Greer, *Texas Ranger*, 130.
27. Robinson, *Men Who Wear the Star*, 87; Wilkins, *Highly Irregular Irregulars*, 75; Bauer, *Mexican War*, 90; Clayton and Chance, *March to Monterrey*, 63.
28. Wilkins, *Highly Irregular Irregulars*, 75; Bauer, *Mexican War*, 90; Clayton and Chance, *March to Monterrey*, 63.
29. W.H. King, "The Texas Ranger Service," in D.G. Wooten (ed.), *Comprehensive History of Texas*, II:338; Bishop, Curtis, "Colt Pistol Work," *Frontier Times* (Summer 1961): 48.
30. Webb, *Texas Rangers in the Mexican War*, 21.
31. Bauer, *Mexican War*, 90; James K. Holland, "Diary of a Texan Volunteer," *Southwestern Historical Quarterly* 30 (July 1926): 25; Greer, *Texas Ranger Jack Hays*, 135.
32. Curtis Bishop, "Colt Pistol Work," *Frontier Times* (Summer 1961): 48; Clary, *Eagle and Empire*, 193; Cutrer, *Ben McCulloch*, 79.
33. James K. Holland, "Diary of a Texan Volunteer," *Southwestern Historical Quarterly* 30 (July 1926): 25.
34. *New Orleans Picayune*, October 23, 1846.

Chapter 8

35. Eisenhower, *So Far from God*, 120; Caperton, Sketch of Colonel John C. Hays," 43; Chamberlain, *My Confession*, 80.
36. Utley, *Lone Star Justice*, 69; Lavender, *Climax at Buena Vista*, 110; Giddings, *Sketches of a Campaign*, 192.
37. Greer, *Texas Ranger Jack Hays*, 138; "Recollections of the Mexican War," by "A Pioneer," in *The Pioneer*, October 15, 1900, 152.
38. Dugard, *Training Ground*, 201.
39. Barry, *Texas Ranger and Frontiersman*, 34.
40. Barry, *Texas Ranger and Frontiersman*, 34; *New Orleans Picayune*, October 23, 1846.
41. Barry, *Texas Ranger and Frontiersman*, 34.
42. Eisenhower, *So Far from God*, 131; Utley, *Lone Star*, 69; Dugard, *Training Grounds*, 202.
43. Greer, *Jack Hays Texas Ranger*, 143.
44. Reid, *Scouting Expedition*, 159.

Chapter 9

45. Spurlin, *Texas Volunteers*, 86; Greer, *Texas Ranger, Jack Hays*, 144; Eisenhower, *So Far from God*, 130.
46. Greer, *Texas Ranger, Jack Hays*, 145.
47. Spurlin, *Texas Volunteers*, 90; Smithwick, *Evolution of a State*, 212; Cox, *Texas Rangers*, 111; Spurlin, *Texas Volunteers*, 90; Webb, *Texas Rangers*, 31; Collins, *Texas Devils*, 27; Greer, *Colonel Jack Hays*, 137.
48. Quoted in Caperton, "Sketch of Colonel John C. Hays," 45.
49. Hays and Caperton, "Jack Hays," 17; Caperton, "Sketch of Colonel John C. Hays," 45.

Chapter 10

50. Barry, *Texas Rangers and Frontiersman*, 38.
51. Dishman, *Perfect Gibraltar*, 186.
52. Collins, *Texas Devils*, 28; Reid, *Scouting Expeditions*, 192; Kendall, *Dispatches from the Mexican War*, 94; Dugard, *Training Ground*, 225.
53. Lee, *Three Years Among Comanches*, 73.
54. Sowell, *Life of "Big Foot" Wallace*, 123.
55. Collins, *Texas Devils*, 28.
56. Cutrer, *Ben McCulloch*, 87.
57. Webb, *Texas Rangers*, 108; Eisenhower, *So Far from God*, 146; terms of the truce were so liberal as to call down on Taylor a storm of protest and criticism; Articles of Capitulation of the City of Monterey, *U.S. House Executive Document 4*, 29th Congress, 2nd session, 102 ff.
58. Greer, *Texas Ranger, Jack Hays*, 152.
59. Urwin, *United States Cavalry*, 82.
60. Greer, *Texas Ranger, Jack Hays*, 153.
61. Cox, *Texas Rangers*, 111; Spurlin, *Texas Volunteers*, 104.
62. Collins *Texas Devils*, 28; *General Taylor and His Staff*, 110.
63. Greer, *Colonel Jack Hays*, 153.
64. Hays and Caperton, "Jack Hays," 17.

Chapter 11

65. Lavender, *Climax at Buena Vista*, 125.
66. Webb, *Texas Rangers*, 111; Wool to Taylor, January 27 and 29, *U.S. House Executive Doc. 60*, 1106.
67. Lavender, *Climax at Buena Vista*, 166.
68. Robinson, *Men Who Wear the Star*, 94; Cutrer, *Ben McCulloch*, 60.
69. Cutrer, *Ben McCulloch*, 92; Utley, *Lone Star Justice*, 76.
70. Webb, *Texas Rangers in the Mexican War*, 66; Cutrer, *Ben McCulloch*, 94; Lavender, *Climax at Buena Vista*, 169.
71. Cutrer, *Ben McCulloch*, 96; Webb, *Texas Rangers in the Mexican War*, 67; Spurlin, *Texas Volunteers*, 254.
72. Webb, *Texas Rangers*, 113.
73. Urwin, *United States Cavalry*, 86.
74. Cutrer, *Ben McCulloch*, 99.
75. Herr and Wallace, *Story of the U.S. Cavalry*, 38; Lavender, *Climax at Buena Vista*, 211.

Chapter 12

76. Reid, *Scouting Expeditions*, 53.
77. Ibid.; Cutrer, *Ben McCulloch*, 73.
78. Hardin, *Texas Rangers*, 15.

Chapter 13

79. Greenberg, *Wicked War*, 132; Barry, *Texas Ranger and Frontiersman*, 40, 42.
80. Cox, *Texas Rangers*, 111.
81. Ibid.; Ford, "John C. Hays in Texas," Ford Papers, 29.
82. Bauer, *Zachary Taylor*, 184.
83. Robinson, *Men Who Wear the Star*, 93; Wilkins, *Highly Irregular Irregulars*, 114.
84. Ford, *Rip Ford's Texas*, 87; Robinson, *Men Who Wear the Star*, 94.

Chapter 14

85. Bauer, *Mexican War*, 221; McCaffery, *Army of Manifest Destiny*, 125; Lavender, *Climax at Buena Vista*, 90.

86. Chance, *Mexico Under Fire*, 174; Livermore, *War with Mexico Reviewed*, 149; Crane, *Life and Select Literary Remains*, 379; Zachary Taylor to the Adjutant General, May 23, 1847, *U.S. House Executive Doc. 60*, 1138; Cutrer, *Ben McCulloch*, 74.

87. Clary, *Eagle and Empire*, 168; *House Executive Doc. 60*, 157; Levinson, *Wars Within*, 68.

88. Clary, *Eagle and Empire*, 168; Elliott, *Winfield Scott*, 448.

89. Collins, *Texas Devils*, 12.

90. Ibid., 13.

91. Lander, *A Trip to the Wars*, 24; Chance, *Mexican War Journal*, 107.

92. Chamberlain, *My Confession*, 202.

93. Smith, *Chile Con Carne*, 261.

94. Collins, *Texas Devils*, 8; Giddings, *Sketches of the Campaign*, 97.

95. Collins, *Texas Devils*, 23; *U.S. House Executive Doc. 60*, 1178; Lane, *Adventures and Recollections*, 56; Webb, *Texas Rangers*, 112.

Chapter 15

96. Lavender, *Climax at Buena Vista*, 280.

97. Chamberlain, *My Confession*, 83.

98. Brown, "Mexican War Experiences of Albert Pike."

Chapter 16

99. Chamberlain, *My Confession*, 176.

100. Smith, *Chili Con Carne*, 294 .

101. Wilkins, *Highly Irregular Irregulars*, 138; Spurlin, *Texas Volunteers*, 272.

102. Giddings, *Sketches of the Campaign*, 325.

103. Collins, *Texas Devils*, 16; Smith, *Chile Con Carne*, 294; Chance, *Mexico Under Fire*, 261; Spurlin, *Texas Volunteers*, 64, 118; Utley, *Lone Star Justice*, 77.

104. Lane, *Adventures and Recollections*, 48.

105. Ibid., 49.

106. Chamberlain, *My Confession*, 269.

107. Lane, *Adventures and Recollections*, 50.

108. Chamberlain, *My Confession*, 61, 267; Ford, *Rip Ford's Texas*, 64; Lane, *Adventures and Recollections*, 57.
109. Lane, *Adventures and Recollections*, 55.
110. Spurlin, *Texas Volunteers*, 121.

Chapter 17

111. Webb, *Texas Rangers in Mexican War*, 115; Oswandel, *Notes on the Mexican War*, 171.
112. Collins, *Texas Devils*, 18.
113. Samuel Walker to Jonathan Walker, June 6, 1847, Walker Papers.
114. Cox, *Texas Ranger Tales*, 8; Greer, *Colonel Jack Hays* 173; Chance, *Mexican War Journal of Captain Franklin Smith*, 150.
115. Clary, *Eagle and Empire*, 382.
116. Collins, *Texas Devils*, 20.

Chapter 18

117. Webb, *Texas Rangers*, 118.
118. Greer, *Texas Ranger, Jack Hays*, 178.
119. Collins, *Texas Devils*, 24; Reid, *Scouting Expeditions*, 107; Frost, *Mexican War*, 305; Ferrell, *Monterrey Is Ours*, 14.
120. Brackett, *General Lane's Brigade*, 173; Ford, *Rip Ford's Texas*, 68; John S. Ford, "Services of Col. John C. Hays," Texas Confederate Museum Collection, Haley Memorial Library and History Center, Midland, Texas.
121. *New Orleans Picayune*, December 29, 1847; Greer, *Colonel Jack Hays*, 181.
122. Webb, *Texas Rangers*, 119; Oates, "Los Diablos Tejanos!," 46. *Los Diablos Tejanos* is Spanish for "the Texas devils."
123. Hays and Caperton, "Jack Hays," 21.
124. Lee, *Three Years among the Comanches*, 74.
125. Collins, *Texas Devils*, 31; Hitchcock, *Fifty Years in Camp and Field*, 310; Webb, *Texas Rangers*, 119.
126. Collins, *Texas Devils*, 32; Ford, *Rip Ford's Texas*, 81; Lee, *Three Years among the Comanches*, 74; Nackman, "Making of the Texan Citizen Soldier," 243.
127. Ford, *Rip Ford's Texas*, 84; Dumont's Letters, published in the *Indiana Register* and quotes in the *Democratic Telegraph and Texas Register*, February 24, 1848.
128. Collins, *Texas Devils*, 32; Ford, *Rip Ford's Texas*, 81; Webb, *Texas Rangers*, 120.

129. Ford, "John C. Hays in Texas," Ford Papers, 29; Herr and Wallace, *Story of the U.S. Cavalry*, 58.
130. Utley, *Lone Star*, 81.
131. Ford, *Rip Ford's Texas*, 81.
132. Collins, *Texas Devils*, 33; Ford, *Rip Ford's Texas*, 81; Lee, *Three Years among the Comanches*, 76; Webb, *Texas Rangers*, 120.
133. Utley, *Lone Star*, 83; Ford, *Rip Ford's Texas*, 89; Hays and Caperton, "Jack Hays," 23.
134. Cox, *Texas Rangers*, 120.
135. Ibid., 121.
136. Hays and Caperton, "Jack Hays," 24.
137. Cox, *Texas Rangers*, 120; Clary, *Eagle and Empire*, 404.

Chapter 19

138. Cox, *Texas Rangers*, 121; Ford, "John C. Hays in Texas," Ford Papers, 72.
139. Cox, *Texas Rangers*, 121.
140. Clary, *Eagle and Empire*, 169
141. Ibid., 367.
142. Ford, *Rip Ford's Texas*, 72; Collin, *Texas Devils*, 12.

Chapter 20

143. Strong, *Stories from Texas*, 57.
144. Ibid., 58.
145. Collins, *Texas Devils*, 23.
146. Ibid., 26; Greer, *Colonel Jack Hays*, 134.

SOURCES

Manuscripts

Caperton, John, "Sketch of Colonel John C. Hays, The Texas Rangers, Incidents in Texas and Mexico, Etc." Center for American History, University of Texas, Austin.

Ford, John S. "John C. Hays in Texas." John Salmon Ford Papers, Center for American History. Memoirs of Archives Manuscripts. University of Texas at Austin.

Walker, Samuel H. Papers. Texas State Library and Archives, Austin.

Government Documents

United States Congress. House of Representatives. 29th Congress, 2nd Session, Serial Set No. 497, H.R. Executive Document 4. Articles of Capitulation of the City of Monterey.

United States Congress. House of Representatives. 30th Congress, 1st Session, Serial Set No. 520, H.R. Executive Document No. 60. Hostilities by Mexico. The message of the President of the United States Relative to an invasion and commencement of hostilities by Mexico, May 11, 1846.

Military and Government Publications

U.S. Army, Center of Military History. "Chapter 8: The Mexican War and After." Accessed April 30, 2022. history.army.mil/books/AMH/AMH-08.htm.

———. CHM PUB 73-3, "The Occupation of Mexico May 1846–July 1848." Accessed September 3, 2022. history.army.mil/catalog/pubs/73/73-3.html.

U.S. House Executive Doc 4. "Articles of Capitulation of the City of Monterey." U.S. Congress. House of Representatives. 29th Congress, 2nd Session. Serial Set No. 497.

U.S. House Executive Doc 60. "Hostilities by Mexico. The message of the President of the United States Relative to an invasion and commencement of hostilities by Mexico, May 11, 1846." United States Congress. House of Representatives. 30th Congress, 1st Session. Serial Set No. 520.

Books

Allen, Desmond Walls. *Arkansas' Mexican War Soldiers*. New York: D.W. Allen, 1988.

Barry, James "Buck." *A Texas Ranger and Frontiersman*. Lincoln: University of Nebraska Press, 1978.

Bauer, K. Jack. *The Mexican War 1846–1848*. Lincoln: University of Nebraska Press, 1992.

———. *Zachary Taylor: Soldier, Planter, Statesman of the Old Southwest*. Baton Rouge: Louisana State University Press, 1993.

Bowman, John S. *Civil War Almanac*. New York: Barnes & Noble Books, 2005.

Brackett, Albert G. *General Lane's Brigade in Central Mexico*. Cincinnati, OH: H.W. Derby and Co., 1954.

Bunting, Josiah, III. *Ulysses S. Grant: The American President*. New York: Henry Holt and Company, 2004.

Butler, Steven R., ed. *A Documentary History of the Mexican War*. Richardson, TX: Descendents of Mexican War Veterans, 1995.

Chamberlain, Samuel. *My Confession: Recollections of a Rogue*. Austin: Texas State Historical Association, 1996.

Chance, Joseph E. *The Mexican War Journal of Captain Franklin Smith*. Jackson: University of Mississippi Press, 1991.

————. *Mexico Under Fire: Being the Diary of Samuel Ryan Curtis 3rd Ohio Volunteer Regiment During the American Military Occupation of Northern Mexico 1846.* Fort Worth: Texas Christian University Press, 1994.

Chapel, Charles Edward. *Guns of the Old West.* New York: Skyhorse Publishing, 2013.

Clary, David A. *Eagle and Empire: The United States, Mexico, and the Struggle for a Continent.* New York: Random House, 2009.

Clayton, Lawrence R., and Joseph E. Chance, eds. *The March to Monterrey: The Diary of Lieutenant Rankin Dilworth, U.S. Army.* El Paso: Texas Western Press, 1996.

Collins, Michael L. *Texas Devils: Rangers & Regulars on the Lower Rio Grande, 1846–1861.* Norman: University of Oklahoma Press, 2008.

Cox, Mike. *Texas Rangers, Wearing the Cinco Peso, 1821–1900.* New York: Tom Doherty Associates, 2008.

————. *Texas Ranger Tales: Stories That Need Telling.* Lanham, MD: Republic of Texas Press, 1997.

Crane, William Carey. *Life and Select Literary Remains of Sam Houston of Texas.* Philadephia, PA: J.P. Lippincott & Company, 1884.

Cutrer, Thomas W. *Ben McCulloch and the Frontier Military Tradition.* Chapel Hill: University of North Carolina Press, 1993.

Dana, Napolean Tecumseh. *Monterrey Is Ours! The Mexican War Letters of Lieutenant Dana 1845–1847.* Edited by Robert H. Ferrell. Lexington: University of Kentucky Press, 2021.

Dilworth, Rankin. *March to Monterrey: The Diary of Lieutenant Rankin Dilworth, U.S. Army: a Narrative of Troop Movements and Observations on Daily Life with General Zachary Taylor's Army During the Invasion of Mexico.* Edited by Lawrence R. Clayton and Joseph E. Chance. El Paso: Texan Western Press, 1996.

Dishman, Christopher D. *A Perfect Gibraltar: The Battle of Monterrey, Mexico, 1846.* Norman: University of Oklahoma Press, 2012.

Dugard, Martin. *Training Ground—Grant, Lee, Sherman, and Davis in the Mexican War, 1846–1848.* New York: Little, Brown, and Company, 2008.

Eckhardt, C.F. *Texas Tales Your Teacher Never Told You.* Latham, MD: Taylor Trade Publishing, 1982.

Eisenhower, John S.D. *So Far From God: The U.S. War in Mexico, 1846–1848.* New York: Random House, 2013.

Elliott, Charles W. *Winfield Scott: The Soldier and the Man.* New York: Macmillan, 1937.

Fehrenbach, T.R. *Comanches; The Destruction of a People.* New York: Alfred A. Knopf, 1974.

Ford, John Salmon. *Rip Ford's Texas.* Edited by Stephen Oates. Austin: University of Texas Press, 1963.

Frost, J. *The Mexican War and Its Warriors: Comprising a Complete History of All the Operations of the American Armies of Mexico.* New Haven, CT: H. Mansfield, 1848.

General Taylor and His Staff: Comprising Memoirs of Generals Taylor, Worth, Wool, and Butler. Philadelphia, PA: Grigg, Elliot and Co., 1848.

Giddings, Luther. *Sketches of the Campaign in Northern Mexico by an Officer of the First Ohio Volunteers.* New York: G.P. Putnam & Co., 1853.

Grant, Ulysses S. *Memoirs and Selected Letters: Personal Memoirs of U.S. Grant; Selected Letters, 1839–1865.* New York: Literary Classics of the United States, 1990.

Greenberg, Amy S. *A Wicked War: Polk, Clay, Lincoln and the 1846 Invasion of Mexico.* New York: Random House, 2012.

Greer, James Kimmins. *Colonel Jack Hays: Texas Frontier Leader and California Builder.* College Station: Texas A&M Press, 1987.

———. *Texas Ranger, Jack Hays in the Frontier Southwest.* College Station: Texas A&M University Press, 1993.

Gulick, Charles A., Jr., Winnie Allen, Katherine Elliott and Harriet Smithers. *Papers of Mirabeau Bonaparte Lamar.* 6 vols. Autin, TX: Von Boeckmann-Jones, 1920–27.

Hardin, Stephen. *Texas Rangers.* New York: Bloomsbury, 2000.

Haynes, Sam W. *Soldiers of Misfortune: The Somervell and Mier Expeditions.* Austin: University of Texas Press, 1990.

Heintzelman, Samuel Peter, and Jerry D. Thompson. *Fifty Miles and a Fight: Major Samuel Peter Heintzelman's Journal of Texas and the Cortina War.* Austin: University of Texas Press, 1998.

Herr, John K., and Edward S. Wallace. *The Story of the U.S. Cavalry.* New York: Bonanza Books, 1953.

Hitchcock, Ethan Allan. *Fifty Years in Camp and Field: Diary of Major General Ethan Allen Hitchcock, U.S.A.* Edited by W.A. Croffut. New York: G.P. Putnam's Sons, 1909.

Hughes, Jeremiah, ed. *Niles' Weekly Register.* Vols. 71–73. Baltimore, MD: Printed by the editor, 1847.

Johnson, Timothy D. *A Gallant Little War: The Mexico City Campaign.* Lawrence: University of Kansas Press, 2007.

Jones, Anson. *Memoranda and Official Correspondence Relating to the Republic of Texas, Its History and Annexation.* New York: D. Appleton and Company, 1859.

Kendall, George Wilkins. *Dispatches from the Mexican War.* Norman: University of Oklahoma Press, 1999.

Kerr, John K., and Edward S. Wallace. *The Story of the U.S. Cavalry 1775–1942.* New York: Bonanza Books, 1953.

Lander, Alexander. *A Trip to the Wars: Comprising the History of the Galveston Riflemen, Formed April 28, 1846, at Galveston, Texas. Together with the History of the Battle of Monterrey; Also, Descriptions of Mexico and Its People.* N.p.: Printed at the Atlas Office, 1847.

Lane, Walter P. *The Adventures and Recollections of General Walter P. Lane, a San Jacinto Veteran: Containing Sketches of the Texian, Mexican, and Late Wars with Several Fights Thrown In.* Austin, TX: Pemberton Press, 1970.

Lavender, David. *The Climax at Buena Vista: The Decisive Battle of the Mexican-American War.* Philadelphia, PA: Lippincott, 1966. Reprint, Philadelphia: University of Pennsylvania Press, 2003.

Lee, Nelson. *Three Years Among the Comanches.* Albany, NY: Baker Taylor, 1859.
———. *Three Years Among the Comanches: The Narrative of Nelson Lee, the Texas Ranger.* Norman: University of Oklahoma Press, 1957.

Levinson, Irving W. *Wars Within Wars: Mexican Guerrillas, Domestic Elites, and the United States of America, 1846–1848.* Fort Worth: Texas Christian University Press, 2005.

Livermore, Abiel Abbot. *War with Mexico Reviewed.* Boston: American Peace Society, 1850.

Lyles, Ian B. *Mixed Blessing: The Role of the Texas Rangers in the Mexican War, 1846–1848.* N.p.: Normanby Press, 2015.

McCaffrey, James M. *Army of Manifest Destiny: The American Soldier in the Mexican War, 1846–1848.* New York: New York University Press, 1992.

Moore, Stephen L. *Savage Frontier: Rangers, Riflemen, and Indian Wars in Texas.* Vol. 4, 1842–45. Denton: University of North Texas Press, 2010.

Moten, Matthew. *Presidents and Their Generals: An American History of Command in War.* Cambridge, MA: Belknap Press of Harvard University Press, 2014.

Newell, Clayton R. *Regular Army Before the Civil War, 1845–1860.* N.p.: Createspace Independent Publisher, 2014.

Oswandel, J.J. *Notes on the Mexican War, 1846–47–48.* Philadelphia, PA, 1885. Reprint, Knoxville: University of Tennessee Press, 2010.

Reid, Samuel C. Jr. *The Scouting Expeditions of McCulloch's Texas Rangers; of the Summer and Fall Campaigns of the Army of the United States in Mexico—1846.* Philadelphia, PA: GG Evens & Co., 1859.

Rickard, J.A. *Brief Biographies of Brave Texans.* Dallas, TX: Hendrick-Long Publishing Company, 1980.

Robart, William Hugh, comp. *Mexican War Veterans: A Complete Roster of the Regular and Volunteer Troops in the War Between the United States and Mexico, 1846 to 1848.* Washington, D.C.: Brentano's, 1887.

Robinson, Charles M., III. *Men Who Wear the Star: The Story of the Texas Rangers.* New York: Random House, 2000.

Samora, Julian. *Gunpowder Justice: A Reassessment of the Texas Rangers.* Notre Dame, IN: University of Notre Dame Press, 1979.

Smith, Justin Harvey. *War with Mexico.* 2 vols. New York: Macmillan Company, 1919.

Smith, S. Compton. *Chili Con Carne: The Camp and the Field.* New York: Miller & Curtis, 1857.

Smithwick, Noah. *Evolution of a State, or, Recollections of Old Texas Days.* Austin, TX: H.P.N. Gammel, 1900. Reprint, Austin: University of Texas Press, 1983.

Sowell, A.J. *Life of "Big Foot" Wallace, the Great Ranger Captain.* Austin, TX: State House Press, 1899.

Spurlin, Charles D. *Texas Volunteers.* Fort Worth, TX: Eakin Press, 1998.

Strong, W.F. *Stories from Texas; Some of Them Are True.* Fort Worth: Berkeley Place Books, Great Texas Line Press, 2018.

Taylor, Zachary. *Letters of Zachary Taylor from the Battlefields of the Mexican War.* Rochester, NY: Genessee Press, 1908.

Urwin, Gregory J.W. *The United States Cavalry: An Illustrated History, 1776–1944.* London: Blandford Press, 1983. Reprint, Norman: University of Oklahoma Press, 2003.

Utley, Robert M. *Lone Star Justice: The First Century of Frontier Defense.* New York: Oxford University Press, 2002.

Webb, Walter Prescott. *Texas Rangers: A Century of Frontier Defense.* Austin: University of Texas Press, 1989.

———. *The Texas Rangers in the Mexican War.* Traverse City, MI: Jenkins Publishing Company, 1984.

Wilkins, Frederick. *Highly Irregular Irregulars: The Texas Rangers in the Mexican War.* Fort Worth, TX: Eakin Press, 1990.

Wilson, R.L. *Colt, An American Legend: The Official History of Colt Firearms from 1836 to the Present.* New York: Abbeville Press, 1985.

Wood, Lamont. *Thornton's Luck: How America Almost Lost the Mexican-American War*. Guilford, CT: Lone Star Books, 2017.

Wooten, Dudley G. *Comprehensive History of Texas 1685–1897*. 2 vols. Edited by William G. Scarff. Dallas: Texas State Historical Association, 1898. Reprint, 1986.

Articles

Bishop, Curtis. "Colt Pistol Work." *Frontier Times* (Summer 1961).

Brown, Jonathan Duff. "Reminiscences of Jon. Duff Brown." *Texas Quarterly State Historical Association* 12 (April 1909).

Brown, Walter Lee. "Mexican War Experiences of Albert Pike and the 'Mounted Devils of Arkansas.'" *Arkansas Historical Quarterly* 12 (Winter 1953).

Hays, Colonel, and Major John Caperton. "Jack Hays, the Intrepid Texas Ranger." *Frontier Times* 4, no. 6 (March 1927).

Holland, James K. "Diary of a Texan Volunteer." *Southwestern Historical Quarterly* 30 (July 1926).

Nackman, Mark, "Making of the Texan Citizen Soldier." *Southwestern Historical Quarterly* 78 (January 1975).

Oates, Stephen B. "Los Diablos Tejanos!" *American West* 2 (Summer 1965).

Pioneer, A. "Recollections of the Mexican War." *The Pioneer* (October 1990).

Miscellaneous

Ford, John S. "Services of Col. John C. Hays." *Texas Confederate Museum Collection*. Haley Memorial Library and History Center, Midland, Texas.

Jennings, Major Nathan A. "Reconnaissance Pull in the Offense: A Mexican-American War Case Study." Real Clear Defense Articles. *Armor Magazine*, November 27, 2019.

Lyles, Ian B. "Mixed Blessing: The Role of the Texas Rangers in the Mexican War, 1846–1848. Master's thesis. University of Texas at Austin, Austin, Texas, 2001.

Norris, David A. "Opening Moves on the Rio Grande: The Relief of Fort Texas." Warfare History Network. Accessed March 2, 2022. warfarehistoynetwork.com/article/opening-moves-on-the-rio-grande.

Wood, Lamont. "Blood on the Border: The Mexican War." History Net. April 10, 2017. Accessed April 4, 2018. historynet.com/blood-border-u-s-mexican-war.

Yoder, Randy L. "Rackensackers and Rangers: Brutality in the Conquest of Northern Mexico, 1846–1848." Master's thesis. Oklahoma State University, Norman, Oklahoma, 2006.

Newspapers

Democrat Telegraph and Texas Register (Columbia and Houston), 1848.
Houston Telegraph and Texas Register, 1846.
New Orleans Picayune, 1846, 1847.
Texas Democrat (Austin) 1846, 1847.

INDEX

ABOUT THE AUTHOR

Willliam Nelson Fox is an avid history buff and a passionate researcher of early Texas history, having an opportunity to travel and research "How Texas Came to Be." He is a longtime resident of Midland and Kerrville, Texas.

Visit us at
www.historypress.com